I
WIN

A Collection of
Arguments from the Classroom

Edited by HERSCHEL GREENBERG

Santa Ana College
Mt. San Antonio College
Chaffey College

Kendall Hunt
publishing company

Cover image © Shutterstock, Inc. Used under license.

Kendall Hunt
publishing company

www.kendallhunt.com
Send all inquiries to:
4050 Westmark Drive
Dubuque, IA 52004-1840

Copyright © 2012 by Herschel Greenberg

ISBN 978-1-4652-0413-4

Table of Contents

Acknowledgements v
Introduction vii
How to Use This Book ix
Essay Terms and Definitions xi

Chapter 1: Euthanasia 1
 "Euthanasia: A Wrong Choice" *by Rosalba Beltran Linares* 3
 "Euthanasia: The Right to Choose" *by Celia Guo* 11

Chapter 2: Immigration 17
 "Immigration is Not Color Blind" *by Eliana Flores* 19

Chapter 3: Animal Rights and the Environment 25
 "Money Guzzling Hybrids" *by Samantha Zayas* 27
 "Animal Experimentation: Whether You Live or the Animals Live" *by Sunny Hung* 33
 "Conserving Land for the Future" *by Robert Williams* 39

Chapter 4: Criminal Justice 45
 "Updating Sex Offender Laws" *by Rachel Roberts* 47
 "Prison System Gets an F" *by Lorena Fernandez* 55

Chapter 5: Teen Suicide 61
 "Teenage Suicide" *by Priscilla Garcia* 63

Chapter 6: Wal-Mart 69
 "The Rights of Workers at Wal-Mart" *by Rachel Roberts* 71
 "Wal-Mart is for Boys, Not Girls" *by Marlene Diaz* 77
 "Wal-Mart: A Benefit to All" *by Yadira Alicia Diaz* 83

Chapter 7: Economics and the Recession 91
 "Economic Mobility" *by Wylie McGraw* 93
 "America Today" *by Yali Zhao* 99
 "The American Family" *by Franchesca Cajigal* 105

Chapter 8: Gun Control   **113**
   "Gun Control Laws Fail" *by Jeffrey Hunt*   115
   "Wanted: Gun Control Laws" *by Lam Nguyen*   121

Chapter 9: Education   **129**
   "Educational Budget" *by Dolores VanGordon*   131
   "The Interdependence of Education and the Economy" *by Jeffrey Hunt*   135
   "Schools in America" *by Michael Gonzalez*   141
   "The Importance of Going to Preschool" *by Juana Juarez*   147
   "The Need for a Standardized Curriculum within English Language
      Programs" *by Alex Rollo*   155

Chapter 10: Internet   **163**
   "The Internet: A Useful Tool" *by Samantha Zayas*   165
   "Why the Internet is Dangerous" *by Alejandra B. Martinez*   169

Chapter 11: Television, Video Games, and Other Media   **175**
   "Media: Is it Really Beneficial?" *by Gabriela Ruiz*   177
   "Video Games: Can They Be Stopped?" *by Alejandra B. Martinez*   183
   "Is Violence in the Media Really 'Bad' for Us?" *by Gabriela Lara*   187
   "Virtually Addicted" *by Brian Zajicek*   193
   "Violence Caused by Video Games" *by Carlos Fuentes*   201

Chapter 12: Obesity   **205**
   "Childhood Obesity" *by Verna Trujillo*   207
   "One, Two, Three, No More Fast Food" *by Samantha Zayas*   215
   "A Government's Role in Overcoming Obesity" *by Kevin Russell*   223
   "Obesity and America Today" *by Wylie McGraw*   229

Chapter 13: The Military   **235**
   "The Fight for Political Freedom" *by Jessica Yazdani*   237
   "Gays in the Military" *by Maggie Le*   243

Acknowledgements

Thank you to all the students whose names appear in this book. The credit belongs to you—you are the ones that worked on these assignments, did the research and took the time to construct a strong, clear argument. This book would not exist without you.

I am very grateful to Kendall Hunt and Ryan Schrodt for allowing me a third opportunity (hat trick) to publish a book. With each book, our relationship grows; for that I am thankful. I appreciate your enthusiasm and the trust you have shown me.

I also want to thank Jason McFaul, my colleague and my friend. Once again, I could not do this without you! As always, your support, encouragement, and trust motivate me each day.

I would like to thank my wife, Kathleen, for all her continued support and encouragement throughout this process. I also want to thank my son, Alexander. Even though he is just a toddler, I am inspired to write books like this so he can learn from them when he is old enough to read. I thank my mom, Roberta, and my mother-in-law, Mary, for coming over several times a week to watch Alexander so I could get work done. I would not have been able to finish this book without both of them watching my son. I thank my dad, Paul, for our many conversations about what "modern" students need in order to succeed in college. And I thank my sister, Marissa, for her cheerful questions about the writing process and listening to the struggles of being a writer.

To all future students—may these essays reveal what is possible when you set your mind to putting your thoughts, and arguments, on paper.

Introduction

My first book, *Knowing the Score: A Guide to Writing College Essays*, became successful because I took a different approach to the normal college textbook. The book focuses on teaching how to write an academic argument essay. However, instead of using professional essays as examples, I used student essays. Professionals follow different rules compared to the academic requirements in my class—I often joke with my students that some professional writers would fail my class! When students are at home, they read these professional writers and try to imitate that style. The real problem derives from the student's inability to see the difference between what I require in the classroom and what a professional is capable of doing. This is why I focused on student essays and paragraphs and used them as examples in my first book. This way, students who read these essays at home have a model to follow. If a student wants to know what an "A" paper looks like, all he/she has to do is open my book and look at an example.

After using *Knowing the Score* for over two years and gathering feedback from students, it has become clear that those student samples are very effective. Many students improve throughout the semester—each essay gets better and their grade goes up. I often ask these students what they did to succeed. The response is usually the same: "I just followed the examples in your book."

So the student samples in my book do work! Then I started thinking: What would happen if I had a textbook with all student essays? What if I constructed a modern "reader," one that uses all student essays and paragraphs?

This new book you hold in your hand is the end result of answering my own questions. I started collecting my student essays (and paragraphs) that scored high in my class. I looked at all of them and chose the ones you see here to be published as a collection. Now, students can use this reader at home and see what it takes to write a "winning" essay.

And that is how the book got its title. I want students to know that an essay is an expression, usually an argument, using the written word. I tell my students to write their essays like they are going to win the argument. All of the topics you see here were discussed in class. First, we brainstorm the topic, which gives everyone a view from all sides of the argument. Then, each student writes his/her own essay, forming an opinion, backed by outside research, about any subtopic within our discussion.

Taken together, these concepts form the perfect title: *I Win: A Collection of Arguments from the Classroom.*

How to Use This Book

A "reader" is typically defined as a book put together by an editor containing works by other authors based on a particular subject—in this case, the subject is English. This reader is a book containing works by authors; however, these authors are students. This book, like most readers, is organized by theme. Within each theme, there are many subtopics, and therefore, many different arguments. The topics are euthanasia, immigration, animal rights, environment, criminal justice, bullying, teen suicide, Wal-Mart, economics, recession, guns, education, Internet, television, video games, obesity, and the military. I tried to pick a wide range of arguments, but I will admit, not all sides are represented here. However, there will be something for everyone in this book.

This book is meant to spark class discussion. Based on these readings, a professor could easily lead a class discussion. The essays and paragraphs can also be assigned as homework. Either way, the goal of this reader is to improve the writing of the students in your classroom. By reading material written by other students, your students will gain the confidence needed to improve their writing.

In addition, each essay ends with a series of questions. These questions can be done at home or in the classroom—either way, the questions are designed to spark a constructive discussion of the essay. The essays are general questions, such as: What kind of claim is being made or what kind of support is being used? The questions will help lead the student to writing his/her own response (in the form of a paragraph or essay, which is up to you). There are lines to write these responses at the end of each essay/paragraph and the pages can be torn out of this book and turned in.

Not all the essays and paragraphs in this reader are perfect. There will be mistakes in these works; some arguments and how they are communicated are stronger than others. This is "ok"—one of the questions at the end of the assignment asks to discuss the strengths and the weaknesses of what was just read. Your students do not have to like what they read, but they should have the tools to critically analyze the work in this book. The ability to discuss these things will make your students better writers.

There are two kinds of assignments in this book. Many of the assignments are traditional essays. They have an introduction, body, and a conclusion, and they vary from shorter five paragraph essays to much longer ten or more paragraph essays. However, other assignments are called "combo" paragraphs. These are two to four paragraphs focusing on one specific argument. These "combo" paragraphs do not contain introductions and conclusions. The topic sentences and focused arguments of each paragraph all connect to a main idea that is clearly argued in the assignment.

All of the essays and "combo" paragraphs contain a Works Cited list of all sources. This can also be used to demonstrate MLA (Modern Language Association) style in the classroom, since many different kinds of sources are used throughout the book. The MLA follows the current 7th Edition rulebook (please note that one essay uses APA [American Psychological Association] style, which is noted in the text).

Ultimately, this reader should be used to demonstrate and model good academic writing mechanics. I want your students to finish reading one of the pieces in this book and be excited to write their own argument. I want them to know what an "A" paper looks like. I want them to read this book and say, "I can write like this too." I want students to enter the conversation from the classroom, and I want them to write like they believe in their argument. I want your student to be able to say, "I win!"

Essay Terms and Definitions

Essay—An essay is made up of three parts: An introduction, the support, and a conclusion.

Argument + Support = Essay

An essay is defined as five or more paragraphs.

Thesis—A thesis is a sentence (or sentences) that tells the reader exactly what you are going to write about in your essay. A thesis is the claim/argument that you are going to prove in your essay. It is the reason your essay exists.

Claim + Why = Thesis

Claim—A claim is your opinion/argument. This is what you are arguing in your thesis.

Claim = Argument = Opinion = Thesis

There are three kinds of claims: **Claim of Value, Claim of Policy,** and **Claim of Fact**.

1. A Claim of Value is an argument based on your moral value system. It uses words like *good/bad, better/worse,* and *right/wrong* in order to show approval/disapproval. This claim is commonly used in compare/contrast essays.
2. A Claim of Policy is an argument based on the need to change or fix a rule, law, or policy. It uses words like *should, must,* and *need* to show these changes. This claim is commonly used in problem/solution essays.
3. A Claim of Fact is an argument based on something that has been proven or something that will be provable. This usually involves statistics of some kind, but anything that can be tested and proven as true or false in the future is a Claim of Fact. It uses words like *will, is, are,* and *does* to make this argument. This claim is commonly used in cause/effect essays.

Introduction—An introduction is designed to hook the reader in order to get him/her interested in your topic. The thesis is set in the introduction (toward the end).

Funnel Method—Start general and move to a specific topic.

Quotation—Start with a quote to hook the reader.

Question—Ask a question (or questions). The answer is the introduction and your thesis.

Startling Statistic—Use a startling piece of information to get the reader hooked.

Short Story—Use a fictional (or real) story to appeal to a reader's emotions.

Definition Method—Use the definition (dictionary) of a word or idea.

Supporting Paragraphs—(A good supporting paragraph is 9–13 sentences. Focus on your argument and communicate your ideas). Use this technique in order to write a well-developed paragraph:

T/S = Topic Sentence (your argument for that paragraph).

EL = Elaborate your topic sentence.

E/Q = Example or Quote for Support. Do not use yourself as support because it cannot be proven! Use outside sources to prove your argument.

A = Analyze the support. Connect it to the T/S or thesis.

C/T = Conclude or transition, based on what you need. A T/S can also contain a transition.

Types of Support:

1. **Factual Evidence based on Statistics**—This is a piece of evidence used as support based on a stat, poll, survey or some kind of empirical data.
2. **Factual Evidence based on Example**—This is a piece of evidence used as support based on a real example. It is something that really happened, but it is not based on stats.
3. **Interpretation based on Expert Opinion**—This is an interpretation of a fact based on someone's expert opinion.
4. **Interpretation based on Causal Connection**—This is an interpretation of a fact based on the cause and effect of two ideas or events.
5. **Interpretation based on Problem/Solution**—This is an interpretation of a fact based on offering solutions to existing (or future) problems.
6. **Interpretation based on Prediction of the Future**—This is an interpretation of a fact based on offering predictions of what will happen in the future based on the subject (and determined by that fact).

Essay Types—There are many types of essays. A good essay combines all the methods needed in order to prove the thesis. All essays have something in common—they are arguments and they require research. The essay types include: **Definition, Process-Analysis, Compare/Contrast, Cause/Effect, Problem/Solution, Literary,** and **Persuasive**.

Counter Argument and Refute Paragraphs—A college essay often includes the counter argument, which is a paragraph that argues against your thesis or a main point in your essay. This is the common argument used against you. However, this counter argument must be refuted; therefore, another paragraph appears after the counter argument in order to prove the counter argument false. The refute paragraph should "destroy" the counter argument. If you do this, the only argument left standing is your own.

Transitions—These are used between sentences and paragraphs. They help tell the reader what you are doing between these sentences and paragraphs. Transitions include:

Addition:
also, again, furthermore, in addition, likewise, moreover, similarly

Consequence:
accordingly, as a result, consequently, for this reason, hence, otherwise, therefore, thus

Exemplifying:
especially, for instance, in particular, namely, particularly, specifically, such as

Illustration:
for example, for instance, as an illustration, in this case

Emphasis:
above all, chiefly, with attention to, especially, particularly

Similarity:
comparatively, likewise, similar, moreover

Contrast and Comparison:
by contrast, conversely, instead, likewise, on one hand, on the other hand, on the contrary, rather, similarly, yet, but, however, still, nevertheless, in contrast

Exception:
aside from, besides, except, excluding, other than, outside of

Restatement:
in essence, in other words, namely, that is, that is to say, in short, in brief

Conclusion—The conclusion is the last paragraph in your essay. It is designed to remind the reader of everything you argued and proved in your essay. To do this, summarize your thesis in one sentence. Then, summarize each supporting paragraph in one sentence. Put this all together in your conclusion in the order they appear in the essay. You can refer back to your hook/theme used in the introduction in your conclusion. Do not introduce any new ideas in the conclusion.

Chapter 1

Euthanasia

Euthanasia (also known as mercy killing) is the act of putting to death without pain, or allowing to die, a person suffering from a painful disease or condition. This can occur by withholding extreme medical measures, or by purposely putting to death an individual who asks for it. Cases like this occur throughout society, and many people feel passionate about whether euthanasia (which can be performed by a doctor or family member) is ethical. The debate centers around the person's right to choose how to die, especially in dire medical situations. In Rosalba Beltran Linares's essay, she argues that euthanasia is unethical and should not be used even when the patient requests it. On the other hand, Celia Guo's combo paragraph argues that euthanasia is a freedom of choice and should be allowed.

Rosalba Beltran Linares
English 101
07-18-11

Euthanasia: A Wrong Choice

Euthanasia is a way for many people to end their life from pain and suffering. It is terrifying when someone mentions the word euthanasia, since some people are scared of dying. Euthanasia, or intended death, is an issue that has been debated for many years. According to an article, Sandra M. Alters states, "The movement to legalize euthanasia in England began in 1935 with the founding of the Voluntary Euthanasia Society. . . . The euthanasia Society of America was established in 1938. In 1967 this group prepared the first living well. Renamed the Society for the Right to Die in 1974" (53). It is hard to comprehend euthanasia since it is a truly sad situation that ends people's life. Physicians might prescribe lethal medication to terminally patients to end their suffering and pain. According to an online article, "Euthanasia and Assisted Suicide: The battle Over Legalization Physician Assisted Suicide", it states, "In November 1994 Oregon voters approved Measure 16 by a vote of 51 to 49 percent, making Oregon the first jurisdiction in the United States to legalize physician-assisted suicide. Under the Death with Dignity Act . . . , (likely to die within six months) may request a prescription for a lethal dose of medication to end his or her life." Many incurable people have ended their own life through euthanasia. Euthanasia should not be practiced on any human, even though some people might be affected by terminal diseases that do not have any cure. It is important that today's society understands that there is not any ethical religion that allows people to kill themselves or with somebody's assistance.

To begin with, euthanasia might stop terminal ill people from enjoying a good quality of life ending. Furthermore, it is important that physicians offer high-quality medication treatments to terminal ill patients in order to avoid euthanasia. According to an article, Nancy Harris says, "The medical profession has an intrinsic moral character which prohibits its members from practicing euthanasia. Traditional professional ethics demand that the physician devote him or herself to healing the sick and to serving the higher good of health and wholeness" (31). As this author shows her opposition toward euthanasia, physicians should suggest hospice to their terminal ill patients as an option of extending their life. Furthermore, hospice provides good compassionate care and support to their patients. According to an article, Christie Aschwanden states, "Hospice provides support for people entering the final stages of their lives, and their families; the world is a medieval term that describes a brief resting place on a long and difficult journey" (E3). As the author of this article states, hospice provides care and good support through the dying process, and a hospice may be the best choice of quality care to patients who are suffering from fatal diseases. If terminal ill patients desire hospice, they might have also time to make their wishes come true.

Furthermore, since euthanasia ends people's life in a short period, some doctors might feel emotionally and psychologically discombobulated from helping terminally patients to end with their pain and suffering. As doctors might feel disconcerted from the situation, some physicians experiment culpability or guilt. For example, Dr. Kenneth R. Stevens states:

> The physician is centrally involved in PAS and euthanasia, and the emotional and psychological effects on the participating physician can be substantial. . . . Doctors describe being profoundly adversely affected, being shocked by the suddenness of death, being caught up in the patient's drive for assisted suicide, having sense of powerlessness, and feeling isolated.

It is hard for a society to determine if doctors might be affected mentally and psychologically from practicing euthanasia to terminal ill patients, since PAS (physician assisted suicide) and euthanasia have affected doctors who surround patients that end their life. The government might find a way to eliminate laws that allow physicians to practice euthanasia and assisted suicide to end the existence for terminal ill persons. According to an article, Dr. Stevens states:

> In 1995-96, 405 Dutch doctors were interviewed regarding their feelings after their most recent case of euthanasia, assisted suicide, life ending without an explicit request, and alleviation of pain and other symptoms with high doses of opioids. The percentage of doctors expressing feelings of discomfort were: 75% following euthanasia, 58% following assisted suicide, 34% following life ending without an explicit request and 18% for alleviation of pain with high doses of opioids.

Though this article shows the statistics from doctors who have been affected emotionally and psychologically from practicing euthanasia, many countries have approved euthanasia as a way of dying process to relief the pain and suffering from a terminal ill person. However, many patients fear this method of dying because they are unable to express their concerns due to the illness or disease affecting their body.

In addition, physicians should boycott euthanasia to any patient because some patients might lose their speech as they have gotten an illness that will not allow them to talk anymore, so many of these patients might need to be protected from those who want to end their lives. For example, Arthur L. Caplan, James J. McCartney and Dominic A. Sisti, argue, "No longer able to speak on her own behalf, Mrs. Schiavo is a defenseless human being with inherent dignity, deserving of our respect, care, and concern. Her plight dramatizes one of the most critical questions we face: To be a truly human society, how should we care for those we may not be able to cure?" (96). Since many people believe that humans deserve respect, everyone must value people's life. It is sad when terminal ill patients do not improve their healing condition, and hospitals and physician might stop nourishing them. According to an article, Rusty Benson, argues:

> Recognized and argued in prestigious publications such as *The Journal of the American Medical Association* and *The New England Journal of Medicine*, the

theory of futile care empowers doctors and hospitals to refuse service to patients they deem unworthy of treatment. Practically, that means patients can be killed by withholding nourishment or treatment, even over the objections of the family.

The author of this article shows that terminal ill patients might die from lack of eating because they might not be able to express their eating difficulties. Relatives should find the way to help their ill loved ones who are in this condition. Moreover, governments and social workers must involve in terminal ill life ending programs as well. Then many sick people might be prevented from dying by euthanasia practice.

However, many people argue that euthanasia is the best option for terminally patients. They say that euthanasia is the way for incurable people to end with their pain and suffering. In addition, people also say that there is no medical treatment to prevent terminal ill people from death, and euthanasia might relieve their agony. According to Gary E. McCuen, the writer states:

It is inhumane, cruel and even barbaric to make a suffering person, whose death is inevitable, live longer than he or she wishes. It is the final decision a person makes. . . . It is necessary for physicians to be the agents of death if the person wants to die quickly, safety, peacefully and nonviolently since the best means to accomplish this is medication that only doctors can prescribe. There is not prohibition against a person killing oneself. (101)

Since the author of this article demonstrates that people should not suffer from their illness, doctors might prescribe lethal medication that might suddenly ends with people's life. Therefore, terminal ill people might end their pain and suffering and can die with dignity. According to Marjorie B. Zucker, who states, "If a patient with an incurable and painful disease begged me to do something to end his agony, my immediate response would be very much the same as if a young unmarried woman who was pregnant should ask me to help her avoid the disgrace of giving birth to a child, by producing an abortion" (37). Since the author of this article infers that people might have the right to end his or her life without any suffer, euthanasia might be the right decision for those who go through terminal diseases. On the contrary, what some people might forget is that life is so valuable and precious.

As life is so valuable and precious, people should avoid ending their own existence through euthanasia. Giving love and support as well to terminally patients, it might relieve their depression and pain caused from their terminal disease. There is no doubt that terminal ill people might be worthy of love from their relatives. According to an article, Arthur J. Dick states, "It is love for one's own life, and that of others, that elicits the perception that a suicide should be prevented, and the love of live should be restored. It is love for one's own life and that of others that helps make us cognizant of the various ways in which the love of life is exhibited as a natural, moral imperative" (93). Since the author of this article mentions how valuable life is, many doctors around the world should avoid euthanasia. It is important that relatives prevent their terminal ill patients from being abused in their dying process. According to Andrea C. Nakaya, she argues:

> Concern over chargers of abuse led the Dutch government to undertake studies of the practice in 1990. . . . For example, 60% of Dutch cases of assisted suicide and euthanasia are not reported. . . . The most alarming concern to arise from the Dutch studies has been the documentation of several thousand cases a year in which patients who have not given their consent have their lives ended by physicians. About a quarter of physicians stated that they had "terminated the lives of patients without an explicit request." (165)

Since this author shows that thousands of patients have not given the authorization to end their life, doctors who might practice euthanasia are violating the value of love that life has merited. It is important that society starts getting involved in programs that shows people how valuable and significant life is.

In conclusion, euthanasia should never be practiced to anyone even though those who suffer from terminal ill condition. It is important that everyone be aware that there is not any ethical power that allows anyone to end people's life by euthanasia. First of all, euthanasia might obstruct terminal ill people from having the opportunity of extend their life, and enjoy their final days. Second, since euthanasia ends people's life so quickly, many doctors and physicians might be affected emotional and psychological from helping terminal ill people to end with their suffering. Third, euthanasia should evade for people who might not be able to express their opposition against dying. Many people may be afraid from dying even though they might be long terminal ill patients who are not capable to communicate their fear to die. However, many people argue that euthanasia is the best way to end people's suffering and pain. They also say that is not ethical to keep terminal ill people living longer to extend their pain and suffering. On the contrary, what many people do not understand is that life is so valuable, so terminal ill patients might deserve living longer, and they might eschew from euthanasia. Since euthanasia has been an issue that affects people's life, many people have ended theirs through this method. As Sandra M. Alters argues that euthanasia started in England in 1935, many people might have died from intended death living their relatives in a deeply pain. As euthanasia ends with people's life so quickly, many people might not have the opportunity to make their whishes come truth. Because life is so precious, everyone in the world should respect it. Finally, people who are diagnostic as terminal ill; they may receive care and support from relatives and friends in order to make their last wishes come true, and to be cared and loved during their final stage.

Works Cited

Alters, Sandra M. "Suicide, Euthanasia, and Physician-Assisted Suicide." *Death and Dying End-Of-Life Controversies.* Farmington Hills: Gale, 2010. Print.

Aschwanden, Christie. "The Help of Hospice: More Patients Use the Service for End-of-Life Care. But what is it?" *Los Angeles Times* 25 Jan. 2010: E3. Print.

Benson, Rusty. "Whose Life is Worth More?: Is your Hospital Quietly Practicing Euthanasia Through 'It Futile Care Polices'." *American Family Association Journal.* Web. 01 Dec. 2010.

Caplan, Arthur L., James, J. McCartney, and Dominic A. Sisti. "Ethics at the End of Life." *The Case of Terry Schiavo.* New York: Prometheus Books, 2006. Print.

Dick, Arthur J. "The Case Against Assisted Suicide." *Life's Worth.* Michigan: William B. Eerdmans Publishing Company, 2002. Print.

"Euthanasia and Assisted Suicide: The Battle Over Legalization Physician Assisted Suicide." *Library Index. Death & Dying.* 2010. Web. 08 Dec. 210.

Harris, Nancy. *The Ethics of Euthanasia.* Farmington Hills: Thompson Corporation, 2005. Print.

McCuen, Gary E. "Ideas in Conflict." *Doctor Assisted Suicide.* Wisconsin: Publications Inc., 1999. Print.

Nakaya, Andrea C. "Opposing Viewpoints." *Terminal Illness.* Farmington Hills: Thompson Gale, 2005. Print.

Stevens, Kenneth R. "Emotional and Psychological Effects of Physician-Assisted Suicide and Euthanasia on Participation Physicians." *Issue in Law & Medicine* 21.3 (2006):187–200 *Academic Search Premier.* Web. 01 Dec. 2010.

Zucker, Marjorie B. "A Documentary History." *The Right to Die Debate.* Westport, London: Greenwood Publishing Group., 1999. Print.

Name: _____

Questions

1. What is the author's main argument? What kind of claim is being made? Is this claim effective for this kind of essay? Explain.

_____

_____

_____

_____

_____

2. Analyze one of the support paragraphs. What kind of support is being used? Is the support effective? Are there any support paragraphs that are not effective?

_____

_____

_____

_____

_____

3. Discuss the introduction paragraph. Does the introduction hook the reader? Is the thesis clear and arguable? Explain.

_____

_____

_____

_____

_____

4. Discuss some of the essay's strengths. What does it do well? Be specific.

5. Does the essay have any weaknesses? Explain. How can these weaknesses be improved?

6. Do you agree or disagree with the author? Why? Be specific by referencing the essay. This answer may be written in the form of your own essay.

Celia Guo
English 1C
1-19-12

Euthanasia: The Right to Choose

Anti-Euthanasia activists believe that any form of euthanasia should be abolished. Organizations such as the Patients Rights Council, Nightingale Alliance, and the American Medical Association (AMA) strongly oppose euthanasia because they believe it will not only depreciate the value of life, but it is also unethical. They also believe that it will lead to an increase in deaths. The AMA states that "Euthanasia is fundamentally incompatible with the physician's role as healer. Patients should not be abandoned once it is determined that cure is impossible" ("Euthanasia"). Critics argue that patients considering euthanasia are suffering from depression as well. As a result, critics view euthanasia as unacceptable because depression is treatable. Dr. David Graham claims that euthanasia also violates the Hippocratic Oath that all physicians must take, which states "I will apply dietetic measures for the benefit of the sick according to my ability and judgment; I will keep them from harm and injustice. I will neither give a deadly drug to anybody who asked for it, nor will I make a suggestion to this effect" (Gamutan). Consequently, by allowing euthanasia, doctors will be forced to violate the Hippocratic Oath which has been a long standing code of ethics that physicians have followed as a moral guideline for thousands of years. Anti-Euthanasia activists believe the immoral act of euthanasia will ultimately reject the value of human life, so it must be eradicated.

By focusing on physician duties, anti-euthanasia activists fail to recognize patient freedoms. The decision to end a life ultimate lies in the hands of the individual, not those around them. In a Supreme Court case regarding euthanasia, it stated that "The right of a competent, terminally ill person to avoid excruciating pain and embrace a timely and dignified death bears the sanction of history and is implicit in the concept of ordered liberty" (Vacco). It is apparent that a person's desire to euthanize themselves is an individual right, so opponents should not have the final judgment in something that is considered to be a private moral law. Throughout the past couple of decades, euthanasia has become more commonly accepted around the world as an acceptable method for relieving pain and suffering. For instance, euthanasia has been legalized in Belgium, Luxembourg, and The Netherlands ("Euthanasia Now Legal in Holland").

In these countries, studies have shown that with the legalization of euthanasia, deaths have not increased. Research has shown that "In countries where euthanasia is legal, there has not been a dramatic increase in cases. In the Netherlands, about 3,800 deaths a year (or about 2.5% of the total) are listed as euthanasia or assisted suicide requests" (Knox). It is evident that legalizing euthanasia will not lead to an increase in deaths, but instead, it increases autonomy. Outlawing euthanasia would also be a violation of the Fourteenth Amendment of the United States Constitution, which states that "No state shall make or enforce any law which shall abridge the privileges or immunities of citizens of the United States; nor shall any state deprive any person of life, liberty, or property." In essence, if individuals have a right to life, it would also mean that individuals have the right to die seeing that death is a part of life. All in all, euthanasia does not devalue human life; instead, it values human freedom.

Works Cited

"Euthanasia." *Issues & Controversies*. Facts On File News Services, 17 May 2010. Web. 18 Jan. 2012.

"Euthanasia Now Legal in Holland." *CNN World*. Cable News Network, 2012. Web. 17 Jan. 2012.

Gamutan, Yolly Eileen A. "The Hippocratic Oath." *Catholic Association of Doctors and Nurses*. Wilmy Designs, 2010. Web. 18 Jan. 2012.

Knox, Noelle. "An Agonizing Debate About Euthanasia." USA Today. *USA Today*, 2008. Web. 17 Jan. 2012.

Vacco v. Quill. 521 U.S. 793. Supreme Court of the United States. 1997. Cambridge University Press. Web. 18 Jan. 2012.

Name: _____

Questions

1. What is the author's main argument? What is the overall claim being made? Explain.

   _____

   _____

   _____

   _____

   _____

2. Analyze one of the paragraphs. What kind of support is being used? Is the support effective?

   _____

   _____

   _____

   _____

   _____

3. Discuss the flow of one of the paragraphs. Is the topic sentence effective? Does the rest of the paragraph match the topic sentence? Explain.

   _____

   _____

   _____

   _____

4. Discuss some of the strengths of this assignment. What does it do well? Be specific.

5. Does the assignment have any weaknesses? Explain. How can these weaknesses be improved?

6. Do you agree or disagree with the author? Why? Be specific by referencing the essay. This answer may be written in the form of your own essay.

Chapter 2

Immigration

Immigration is an ongoing debate in American politics. It covers a wide range of issues, such as immigrant rights, laws that are broken, and social resources used by immigrants. This includes illegal and legal immigrants, and depending on where you live, the arguments can polarize our society. In Eliana Flores's essay, she argues that the United States government is targeting Hispanic immigrants unfairly, and she uses many different types of arguments to help prove her claim.

Eliana Flores
English 68
February 10, 2011

Immigration is Not Color Blind

People today seem to blame immigrants for any issue occurring in the United States. If Americans feel threatened, fingers are pointed at the immigrants. If an American does not have a job, again, fingers are pointed at the immigrants. Because Mexicans make up the majority of the immigrants in the U.S., Americans are growing a strong resentment towards Mexicans. This sentiment can be seen in the current notions and measures that are being created by the United States. The government and the media are aiming various policies to discriminate against the Mexican immigrants. Since Mexicans are by no means white (for the most part), the U.S. is purposely practicing these acts to keep the Mexicans from dissolving the white identity of the country.

The U.S.-Mexico Border Fence is a symbol that illustrates the anti-immigrant sentiment towards Mexicans. The building of a wall, specifically in the border line with Mexico, makes the government appear to be racially discriminating against Mexicans. The principles of the U.S. have been put aside and many Americans do not realize that there is indeed a growing hatred against Mexican immigrants. For example, the purpose of the U.S.-Mexico Border is to prevent the entrance of illegal immigrants (Gibson). The government seems to believe that immigrants only come from Mexico and not other places, such as Canada. Nonetheless, if securing the borders were truly the intentions of the government, then why does the government not secure the Canadian border? The Canadian border is approximately 5, 500 miles in length, whereas the Mexico border is hardly 2, 000 miles ("US-Canada and US-Mexico Border Lengths"). It would make sense that since the Canadian border is almost three times greater than the Mexican border, there would be more security in the border with Canada. However, only 32 miles of the Canadian border are actually being secured ("Only 32 Miles of US-Canada Border are Secure"). The reason for this is because Canadians are light skinned and Mexicans are not. Apparently it is okay for illegal Canadian immigrants to cross the border because they are the color of the majority in the U.S.—white. Point proven, the U.S.-Mexico Border Fence serves as merely an excuse to legally and indirectly discriminate against Mexican immigrants, thus showing that the U.S. has the concept that being "white is right."

Similarly, the SB 1070 is another example that proves that the United States discriminates against any group who is threatening the white culture of the country. This law is most definitely a form of racial profiling and it is also a legal way for U.S. authorities to harass all Hispanics (which are mostly Mexicans). As a case in point, this law requires police to demand documents proving citizenship and putting to jail anyone who cannot prove so ("Racial Profiling, SB 1070 Will Go Hand in Hand"). Coincidently, the targets of this law are Hispanics. If a person sounds or looks Hispanic, authorities have the right to question their citizenship ("Racial Profiling, SB 1070 Will Go Hand in Hand").

Whether a person is a legal or illegal resident, he or she can go to jail for not proving citizenship. The reason behind this act is to protect America from violent immigrants, or even worse, terrorists. However, why do those of Hispanic complexions have to be the target? Is it not possible for a person of light skinned color to be a threat? It is possible, but it is simply easier to blame a minority group because they are not part of the White majority. This law, therefore, illustrates the prejudice against Hispanics, made up mostly by Mexicans.

Because of the magnitude of the actions that have been taken by the government, myths of great magnitude have also been created by the news, which, ironically, mostly support the government. The fallacies of these myths are made to be seen so real that they have been engraved into people's minds. For example, one myth that people constantly talk about, according to Aviva Chomsky, a professor of Latin American studies, is that immigration is a problem (166). This came to be believed true because of how the government and the media exaggerate about immigration. They purposely make Americans think of immigration as a huge problem that needs to be stopped. The problem includes that immigrants steal jobs, threaten security, and many other fallacies. However, immigration is not a problem for these reasons.

Immigration is not a problem in terms of how people define the actual problem. The real problem is a humanitarian problem, but many people are not aware of this issue. According to Aviva Chomsky, the measures taken to regulate, or end, immigration is what makes immigration a humanitarian problem (166). The U.S. policies create global inequality because of the cheap source of labor it depends on in other countries. Because of this exploitation, people from such countries start immigrating and thus another humanitarian problem arises—border enforcements. Border enforcements have caused thousands of deaths and injuries (Chomsky 166). In essence, immigration is a problem, but not the kind of problem that people think it is. And again, this myth is so prominent because of how negative the government and media portray immigrants.

In conclusion, the U.S. government's system is unjustly discriminating against what is now the majority of the immigrants—Mexicans. The U.S. Mexico Border Fence is a great example that illustrates Americans' repugnance towards Mexican immigrants. The SB 1070 also serves to demonstrate that the U.S. is intentionally picking on Mexican immigrants. Additionally, as if it were not enough, these policies that the government is following are allowing for myths to exist, which add to the anti-immigration resentment towards Mexicans. This, again, is happening to help keep the dominant group in power and conserve the country's white identity.

Works Cited

Chomsky, Aviva. *They Take Our Jobs and Twenty Other Myths About Immigration.* Boston, Massachusetts: Beacon Press, 2007. Print.

Gibson, R. Sebastian. "Discrimination Against Hispanics, Latinos and Mexican Americans, and the Need For More Civil Rights Lawyers in California." *HG.org.* HG.org, 8 Feb, 2009. Web. 4 Feb. 2011.

"Only 32 Miles of US-Canada Border are Secure." *NWCN.COM.* Northwest Cable News, Inc., 8 Feb. 2011. Web. 8 Feb. 2011.

"Racial Profiling, SB 1070 Will Go Hand in Hand." *Arizona Daily Star.* Arizona Daily Star, 16 Apr. 2010. Web. 8 Feb. 2011.

"US-Canada and US-Mexico Border Lengths." *U.S. Census Bureau*, Statistical Abstract of the United States: 2011. U.S. Census Bureau, Statistical Abstract of the United States: 2011, 2011. Web. 9 Feb. 2011.

Name: _____

Questions

1. What is the author's main argument? What kind of claim is being made? Is this claim effective for this kind of essay? Explain.

_____

_____

_____

_____

2. Analyze one of the support paragraphs. What kind of support is being used? Is the support effective? Are there any support paragraphs that are not effective?

_____

_____

_____

_____

3. Discuss the introduction paragraph. Does the introduction hook the reader? Is the thesis clear and arguable? Explain.

_____

_____

_____

_____

4. Discuss some of the essay's strengths. What does it do well? Be specific.

5. Does the essay have any weaknesses? Explain. How can these weaknesses be improved?

6. Do you agree or disagree with the author? Why? Be specific by referencing the essay. This answer may be written in the form of your own essay.

Chapter 3

Animal Rights and the Environment

Does your pet have rights? Do animals in a science lab have rights? Are hybrid engines better than gasoline engines when it comes to the environment? These issues are addressed in this chapter. Animals and the environment affect people everyday, and arguments abound for both. First, Samantha Zayas will argue that hybrid cars are not better than normal cars. Clearly, the result of this argument can have an impact on the environment. Next, Sunny Hung discusses whether animals have rights, especially those used in medical, pharmaceutical, and make-up industries. Finally, Robert Williams discusses the land itself, arguing about land conservation and its impact on the future.

Samantha Zayas
English 68
February 10, 2011

Money Guzzling Hybrids

Hybrid cars, a recent innovation to the car industry, are losing to traditional gasoline powered vehicles in saving consumers money by being fuel-efficient. With gas prices reaching almost four dollars a gallon, many people are in search for quick, inexpensive transit. Nevertheless, do hybrids save people money by consuming less fuel? The answer is no, at least not a significant amount of money. Some people might save a few hundred dollars a year, driving a hybrid for short distances, in a causal manner, and in the city. However, while that may be some people, most Americans are going to have difficulty conserving money from hybrid technology because of their driving style, which is often aggressive and includes long distances at high speeds. To understand the reasoning why this is the case, it is necessary to know that hybrid cars have two engines, instead of one as in the conventional automobiles. The battery engine of a hybrid works while the person is driving at or below forty miles per hour. As soon as the person exceeds forty miles per hour, the gasoline motor begins to work, and the other engine gradually turns off. Depending on the driving style of the driver, the gas engine in a hybrid can be used more than the battery motor. As previously stated, most Americans demand much from their automobiles, when it comes to performance. Hence, many people may fill up their gasoline tank as often as they would if they drove a conventional vehicle. According to *Consumer Reports*, an organization centered on discovering the benefits and drawbacks of products purchased by consumers, " . . . we found some models that will cost you more to own than a conventional equivalent at any gas price on record" ("Hybrids & diesels: Do they save money?"). The price of fuel would have to be astronomically high in order for people to begin saving money. Hybrid cars are not the best fuel-efficient cars because they can burn as much gas as traditional cars. Essentially, the battery motor of hybrids is primarily used when the car is idling. Possibly, a casual driver—the person driving at or near forty miles per hour—might be able to save some money driving a hybrid. However, most drivers are not laid-back, and they enjoy using the power of their car. Therefore, the fuel engine of a hybrid is going to be used more than the battery motor. As a result, owning hybrids may not be the fuel saving vehicles one may think they are.

In addition, hybrid cars are not money saving vehicles because they have high repair costs. With the economy at a lingering crawl and tight budgets with barely a positive balance, many Americans do not have extra and/or available money to spend on their car's large repair bills. Such bills can vary in price from a few hundred to several thousand dollars. Hybrid cars have an extremely intricate operating system; therefore, their repair costs are more than that of their counterpart, gasoline powered cars. For example, the battery of any hybrid eventually burns out, and on most occasions, the warranty is likely to have expired. The cost to replace the hybrid's battery can range anywhere from one thousand to six thousand dollars. Meanwhile, in a conventional automobile, the ranging cost to replace a dead battery is from forty-five to two hundred fifty dollars. There is a dramatic difference between the replacement of a hybrid battery to a traditional battery, and many people cannot afford to pay the former. In a report done by *Newsweek*, the second largest weekly news magazine in the United States, there is a factual story of a Prius owner whose hybrid car battery had died. According the article, "Philip Card of Utica, N.Y., says a Toyota dealer wanted to charge him $3,900 to replace the battery on his 2001 Prius, which had 350,000 miles on it when he bought it used on eBay this year for $4,357" (Naughton). Even though the battery is the piece of machinery that may aid drivers in saving gasoline, its price tag for replacement is expensive. If there is any money saved from the unpurchased gas, it is subsequently spent on purchasing a new battery. In the article, the dealer gave the owner of the hybrid car the option to either pay ninety percent of the outdated car's purchased value or not replace the dead battery. Card chose not to replace the battery, and many drivers would probably have made the same decision. Most Americans cannot afford to pay such a high price on a car repair, especially when they are on a tight budget. As a result, hybrid cars do not make as economic sense when one has to make car repairs.

Works Cited

"Hybrids & diesels: Do they save money?" *ConsumerReports.org*. Consumers Union of U.S., Inc., 2011. Web. 7 Feb. 2011.

Naughton, Keith. "Assaulted Batteries." *Newsweek*. Harman Newsweek LLC., 2011. Web. 7 Feb. 2011.

Name: _____

Questions

1. What is the author's main argument? What is the overall claim being made? Explain.

_____

_____

_____

_____

_____

2. Analyze one of the paragraphs. What kind of support is being used? Is the support effective?

_____

_____

_____

_____

_____

3. Discuss the flow of one of the paragraphs. Is the topic sentence effective? Does the rest of the paragraph match the topic sentence? Explain.

_____

_____

_____

_____

_____

4. Discuss some of the strengths of this assignment. What does it do well? Be specific.

5. Does the assignment have any weaknesses? Explain. How can these weaknesses be improved?

6. Do you agree or disagree with the author? Why? Be specific by referencing the essay. This answer may be written in the form of your own essay.

Sunny Hung
English 1C
1-19-12

Animal Experimentation: Whether You Live or the Animals Live

A number of animal rights activists suggest that animal experimentation is unethical, as most tested animals would experience excessive pain and side effects from the testing. Since such testing often requires the injection of viruses into the animals' bodies in order to test the efficiency and safety of the medicine on human beings, the failure of the medicine in functioning properly would result in severe damage to the health of the animals and can even result in death. Even though the tested medicine is proved efficient to cure the disease implemented to the animals, the side effect, which constitutes the safety factor of the medicine, is often affecting its own health or even causing unusual genetic changes that could also affect the offspring of the animals. According to the statistics regarding animal experimentation by the U.S. Department of Agriculture, Animal and Plant Health Inspection Service in 2010, 1.13 million animals used in experiments (excluding rats, mice, birds, reptiles, amphibians, and agricultural animals used in agricultural experiments), plus an estimated 100 million mice and rats ("Animal Experiments: Overview"). In addition, according to the science journalist Madhusree Mukerjee, in one of her articles on Scientific American titled "Speaking for the Animals: A Veterinarian Analyzes the Turf Battles That Have Transformed the Animal Laboratory," 76,001 of those testing animals were subjected to pain without pain relief ("Animal Experiments: Overview"). Both statistics above show that there is a huge amount of tested animals every year, and the experimentalists are not treating most of them ethically. Consequently, those tested animals become the sacrifices behind our scientific development. Ironically, all these developments were initially attempting to make our society better, but we neglect all the other creatures that live around us, who share the same environment. Those experimentations on animals are not only inhumane to tested animals but also selfish. As a result, because of the negative impacts on both the tested animals and our environment, all animal experimentations should be banned under the passage of new legislation, and this is what the animal rights activists have fought for during the last couple of decades.

The view on animal testing above only focuses on the morality behind the testing, while they are neglecting the scientific breakthroughs that are brought to attention by those experimentations. Although the claim by those animal rights activists of protecting the tested animals from further harm is sound, but they certainly miss out the essential purpose of these types of testing. Even with all the technological advancement nowadays, still no close substitute could match the contribution of animal testing and its significance to society. According to Pro-test, an Oxford-based group campaigning in favor of continued animal testing, the most distinguishable scientific achievement by animal testing includes the smallpox from the experimentation on cattle: "The vaccine against smallpox was derived from the cowpox virus used by Edward Jenner following his observation that farm workers who contracted cowpox were protected against smallpox - It has now been eradicated from earth" ("Benefits"). Within their website, the organization has also pointed out many other scientific discoveries like the treatment of polio, tuberculosis, typhus, and so on. Despite the fact that all these great scientific discoveries are generated from animal experimentation, opponents still argues that many alternative ways could lead to the same discoveries. To address this issue, *Times* magazine's writer Laura Blue argues that medications must be tested by using a living entity, and scientists need to examine the effect on all of the organs in that living entity. Blue believe that this is the reason we use animals—their biological systems help us determine the effects of these medications. The above views show that the testing of certain medicine requires the qualification in two categories: efficiency and safety. The efficient part of the testing is usually not a problem for modern scientists to figure out, while the safety part is what makes them have headaches all the time. If animal experimentation is banned, scientists could only test the medicine with theoretical approach; they will be faced with many unsolvable problems because the complex human body is not fully understood by the scientist. As a result, if animal experimentation is not permitted as a way to test the new medicines, the advocates of banning animal experimentation seem to suggest that we should go with the human experimentation directly, which usually is the very last step of any modern drug testing. In addition, even though we are still highly dependent on animal testing, the number of experimentations carried is believed to have been reduced, as we know our body much better based on those previous experimentations, and the tested animals would suffer less as society realizes the balance between morality and the importance behind the testing. As a result, animal experimentations truly have its significance and irreplaceable status on various scientific researches, and it should be continued in the means of societal benefits.

Works Cited

"Animal Experiments: Overview." *People for the Ethical Treatment of Animals*. PETA, 2012. Web. 16 Jan. 2012.

"Benefits." *Pro-Test: Standing up for Science*. Pro-Test. Web. 18 Jan. 2012.

Blue, Laura. "How Much Does Animal Testing Tell Us?" *TIME*. Time Inc., 17 June 2008. Web. 16 Jan. 2012.

Name: _____

Questions

1. What is the author's main argument? What is the overall claim being made? Explain.

   _____

   _____

   _____

   _____

   _____

2. Analyze one of the paragraphs. What kind of support is being used? Is the support effective?

   _____

   _____

   _____

   _____

   _____

3. Discuss the flow of one of the paragraphs. Is the topic sentence effective? Does the rest of the paragraph match the topic sentence? Explain.

   _____

   _____

   _____

   _____

4. Discuss some of the strengths of this assignment. What does it do well? Be specific.

5. Does the assignment have any weaknesses? Explain. How can these weaknesses be improved?

6. Do you agree or disagree with the author? Why? Be specific by referencing the essay. This answer may be written in the form of your own essay.

Robert Williams
English 68
6-13-11

Conserving Land for the Future

Theodore Roosevelt, a former U.S President and land conservationist once said, "There can be nothing in the world more beautiful than the Yosemite, the groves of giant sequoias and redwoods, the Canyon of the Colorado, the Canyon of the Yellowstone, the Three Tetons; and our people should see to it that they are preserved for their children and their children's children forever, with their majestic beauty all unmarred" (National Parks Service). This magnificent statement signifies how remarkable President Roosevelt was, but his actions made him even more extraordinary. His presidency led to the creation of the national forest system and the preservation of over 150 million acres (Theodore Roosevelt Association). The United States needs to mimic the policies of Theodore Roosevelt and conserve more land to save the human population from the devastation of development. Conservation and management of preserved land will out weigh the impact of development and destroyed ecosystems, which will ultimately devastate the country and the world.

The protection of the ecosystems in the U.S is the most important factor in keeping the country beautiful and beneficial to its citizens. Life, food, and the climate depend on the delicate ecosystems to provide biodiversity. "Biodiversity" is defined as "Biological diversity in an environment as indicated by numbers of different species of plants and animals." This proves that without the proper amount of land, plants and animals will not be present and the delicate ecosystems can be destroyed. Animals and plants will begin to die and sources of food in the U.S will begin to disappear. Conserving land should be a priority and should be taking place all over the country. If this is not done, habitats will be lost, animals will no longer be able to breed, and plants will have nowhere to grow. Conserving land will help promote biodiversity and in return keep the U.S a healthy and safe place for its citizens. Protecting the ecosystems will not only help the American population, but will also help the rest of the world. Healthy ecosystems will present outdoor recreational activities for the public to enjoy.

Conserving land will protect historical sites, forests, and urban parks. The need to keep these natural landmarks is crucial to the way of life because nature has a way of keeping people in a healthy emotional and physical condition. In other words, the natural beauty of U.S keeps people happy; this is why people travel the country to see spectacular scenery. Professor John Davis of Naropa University and author of *Psychological Benefits of Nature Experiences* wrote, "Exercise and increased physical fitness associated with most kinds of nature-based activities also leads to better mental health." This means hiking through a forest, climbing a mountain, and playing in an urban park will reduce depression and will motivate people to remain healthy. Davis also wrote, "Natural environments provide opportunities for affiliation, social support, intimacy, and group bonding." In this statement, Davis assures that nature provides comfort and offers a place for friends and families to gather. The benefit of nature can only be helpful if land is preserved and if hunting is allowed before self destruction takes place.

Hunting should be allowed on conserved land in order to keep a balance in the delicate ecosystems. There are several species that thrive with land conservation, but some starve and die. Deer and elk are some of the species that will not be able to regulate their own herds. This is due to the lack of natural predators in the country. Wolves, coyotes, and mountain lions are the most common natural predators in the U.S and they regulate herds by eating them. In a book regarding mule deer in North America, it reported, "Approximately three deer are killed a month by mountain lions" (Curtis). This is enough to keep a balance on conserved land, but mountain lions not only threaten deer, but the human population as well. Many of the lions have been hunted down and are nearing extinction. Without predators, deer will begin to overpopulate conservation areas. They will begin to eat all the food in their habitat, and starve to death. Without natural predators and human hunters, the conserved land in the U.S could potentially destroy itself. Hunters are needed in the U.S and land conserved should be accessible to them. Hunting is also a source of food for many and has been for thousands of years. For example, the loss of land will affect Indian tribes in Alaska and could ultimately starve the tribes to death. *CBS News* reports "Alaska's Gwich'in Indians fear that proposed oil drilling on caribou calving grounds could end their ancient culture" (Gildart). The loss of land to oil drilling will disrupt caribou migration and will leave the Gwich'in Indians searching for food in desolate conditions. Not conserving habitats like the ones in Alaska will ravage the country and kill whole groups of people.

Many argue the population of the United States is increasing and the need to develop is essential. People need a place to reside and eat. Homes, stores, and schools are required where ever people live and creating these buildings requires the loss of some land to development. However, home developers do not think this will be disastrous like many conservationists believe it will be. KB Home's current slogan "Environmentally Conscious No Cost Option" is believed to be beneficial to the environment and the residents that live in the homes. KB Home has created an Energy Performance Guide (EPG) that ensures buyers that KB Homes is not an insensitive developer and is trying to protect the planet. Also, there are roughly 309 million people in the U.S, and somehow food needs to be provided to each and every American. In order to do this, land needs to be turned into farms and ranches. This does not require building large homes or factory builds, but instead the land will be used to grow crops and will allow cattle to graze. According to the Vegetable Growers News, "The 2007 Census counted 2,204,792 farms in the United States, a net increase of 75,810 farms from 2002. It listed the number of acres at 922,095,840." This may seem like a large amount of land has already been converted into farmlands, but it is not nearly enough to feed the ever growing U.S population. A lot more land needs to be used to ensure the Americans have a place to live and enough food to survive.

Although this argument is a sensible one, it does not look ahead to the future. The U.S population is growing, but it does not give the right to anyone to destroy land. Former President Theodore Roosevelt once said, "Conservation means development as much as it does protection. I recognize the right and duty of this generation to develop and use the natural resources of our land; but I do not recognize the right to waste them, or to rob, by wasteful use, the generations that come after us" (Prince Williams Conservation Alliance). Roosevelt was the country's leading conservationist and in this quote he tells the people that development is needed, but it cannot be wasteful. Future children should be able to see the beauty of the country. Creating millions of homes, too big for a single family is wasteful and should not be allowed. "Conservation means development as much as it does protection." Home builders take the wrong meaning from this part of Roosevelt's quote. Just like KB Home, one of the largest home builders in California. KB is trying to build a false standard in the industry. The so called Energy Performance Guide is worthless and is only used by KB. They set their own standards and say their homes are perfect. Buyers have reported to ConsumersAffairs.com, "KB is very deceptive" and "KB homes tell you only what you want to hear." Home builders can lie to the public all they want, but the truth is all over the internet. Development is needed, but it needs to be controlled and not wasteful, just as Roosevelt would have wanted.

In conclusion, the people of the U.S need to help support the fight for land conservation in the country. Promoting biodiversity and allowing nature to thrive is in the nation's best interest. The beauty of the scenic countryside's, valleys, and mountains is beneficial to all people that see them. Natural environments will save lives. Hunting is also a long lasting tradition in America. It helps regulate species of animals that over populate without natural predators. Although development is needed to assist the overgrowing population, it has to be controlled and not over destructive. Millions of lives and the outlook of the U.S depend on preserving land. If it is not protected now, then the children of the future will have to live in the devastation.

Works Cited

"biodiversity." *Merriam-Webster.* Merriam-Webster, Incorporated. Web. 30 May 2011.

Consumeraffairs.com. "Consumer Complaints & Reviews." *Consumeraffairs.com.* Consumeraffairs.com, 07 Jan. 2011. Web. 29 May 2011.

Curtis, Sam. *The Complete Guide to Mule Deer Hunting.* Guilford, Connecticut: The Lyons Press, 2003. Print.

Davis, John. "Psychological Benefits of Nature Experience: Research and Theory." *John V. Davis.* Johnvdavis.com. Web. 30 May 2011.

Gildart, Ben. "Hunting for their future: Alaska's Gwich'in Indians fear that proposed oil drilling on caribou calving grounds could end their ancient culture." *BNET.* CBS Interactive. Web. 31 May 2011.

KB Home. "KB Home Energy." *KB Home.* KB Home. Web. 31 May 2011.

National Parks Service. "Theodore Roosevelt Quotes." *nps.gov.* National Parks Service, 28 Dec. 2010. Web. 31 May 2011.

Prince Williams Conservation Alliance. "Conservation, nature & smart growth quotes in no particular order." *Prince Williams Conservation Alliance.* Prince Williams Conservation Alliance. Web. 31 May 2011.

Theodore Roosevelt Association. "National Forest." *Conservationist.* Theodore Roosevelt Association. Web. 31 May 2011.

Vegetable Growers News. "More Farms, Fewer Acres Among U.S. Ag Trends." *VGN.* Great American Publishing. Web. 30 May 2011.

Name: _____

Questions

1. What is the author's main argument? What kind of claim is being made? Is this claim effective for this kind of essay? Explain.

   _____

   _____

   _____

   _____

2. Analyze one of the support paragraphs. What kind of support is being used? Is the support effective? Are there any support paragraphs that are not effective?

   _____

   _____

   _____

   _____

3. Discuss the introduction paragraph. Does the introduction hook the reader? Is the thesis clear and arguable? Explain.

   _____

   _____

   _____

   _____

4. Discuss some of the essay's strengths. What does it do well? Be specific.

5. Does the essay have any weaknesses? Explain. How can these weaknesses be improved?

6. Do you agree or disagree with the author? Why? Be specific by referencing the essay. This answer may be written in the form of your own essay.

Chapter 4

Criminal Justice

Those that commit crimes often find themselves in prisons. The original goal of a prison system was to deter crime; if you do not want to go to prison, do not commit the crime. Today, our prisons are crowded, and many have begun to ask whether they are effective using their current policies. In Rachel Roberts's essay, she discusses sex offender laws as they currently stand. Some of the laws, Rachel argues, are confusing and cause problems in the criminal justice system. Sex offender laws must be clarified in order to improve the system. In Lorena Fernandez's essay, she argues that prisons today are not effective, and changes are needed to make the prison system effectively house an entire population of criminals.

Rachel Roberts
English 101
6-27-2011

Updating Sex Offender Laws

One in five girls and one in ten boys will be sexually victimized before they reach the age of 18 ("2009 Annual Report"). An estimated 115 children are kidnapped and murdered or taken with the intention to be kept, every year in America ("2009 Annual Report"). The fact is, America's children are not protected from the potential danger of sex offenders. The laws written to protect the nation were composed following extreme cases of sexual abuse that were being mourned across America, resulting in ineffective restrictions. Sex offender laws in place today are not only confusing the public on who is truly dangerous but also causing enormous amounts of homeless offenders. Americans are living with a false sense of security and putting their children's safety in laws that tragically, are not serving their purpose.

The sex offender laws in place today were caused by the rare, extremely horrific, child sexual abuse cases sensationalized across America. According to the National Center for Missing and Exploited Children, there are over 620,000 registered sex offenders ("2009 Annual Report"). Eight out of ten sex offenders admit their victims were under the age of 18 (Waymire). These statistics are extremely startling and cause for much concern across the nation. Unfortunately, besides just frightening statistics, many infamous cases of terrible sexual abuse and murder have been the center of news over the past years, including the deaths of Megan Kanka and Jessica Lunsford. In July of 1994, 7-year-old Megan Kanka was raped and murdered after visiting a neighbor and his puppy—it was later discovered that Megan's killer was a two-time convicted child molester ("Megans Law, Registered Sex Offenders And Background Checks"). In February of 2005, 9-year-old Jessica Lunsford was raped and buried alive after being abducted from her home—it was later discovered that Jessica's killer was a known sex offender ("The Jessica Lunsford Tragedy That Resulted In Jessica's Law"). Of course, these cases filled the nation with fear, anger, and sadness—leading to two new laws that would forever change the nation.

Most Americans, including politicians, would agree that sex offender laws in place today were created to protect the American public and their children, after horrifying crimes became an all too common story on the national news. Politicians argued passing more laws would make communities safer by requiring tougher punishments and easier ways to track sex offenders, making them less likely to commit another crime. The horrific murders of Megan Kanka and Jessica Lunsford inspired two laws that politicians believed would forever minimize the danger of sex offenders in America. In 2005, legislators in Florida wrote the Jessica Lunsford Act, which increased the punishment of registered sex offenders that included placing severe restrictions on where they could live ("The Jessica Lunsford Tragedy That Resulted In Jessica's Law"). By passing this law, politicians believed Americans would feel and ultimately, be safer—and the law's idea was that predators would think twice before committing another crime. In 1996, President Clinton signed into affect, Megan's Law, which requires states to have some sort of registry of nearby sex offenders accessible to the public ("Megans Law, Registered Sex Offenders And Background Checks"). Politicians and experts believed that by having sex offenders register, families would be able to protect themselves better and be more aware of their surroundings. Experts also believed that Megan's Law would offer an easier way for law enforcement to track the dangerous predators out on parole or probation. These two laws were written and passed in an effort to make Americans safer and sex offenders less likely to commit new offenses.

The Jessica Lunsford Act is not doing what it was designed to do. This law is causing an extreme amount of sex offenders to become homeless, which in turn makes it difficult—if not impossible—for police to monitor offender's activities and addresses. Under the Jessica Lunsford Act, also known as "Jessica's Law," offenders and predators cannot live within 2000 feet to a school, park, or church. Although the concern of whether sexual predators find housing may seem trivial to most Americans, it is in fact crucial in relation to child safety. What the law does not control is where sex offenders spend their time during the day. Dan Noyes, the Chief Investigative Reporter for *ABC7 News*, interviewed an anonymous, homeless sex offender on whether the Jessica Lunsford Act restricts where he can spend his days and the offender explained, "No, there isn't. You can in fact go from park to park all day long, spending two hours at each of them." Essentially, he is stating that the law politicians rushed so fast to pass, only concerned where a registered sex offender slept, rather than where he or she spent their day. To put it bluntly, a sexual predator can spend all day outside a preschool or park, as long as they sleep a certain amount of feet away—this law does not make Americans and their children safer. According to Wendy Koch of *USA Today*, "Two-thirds of the states allow convicted sex offenders, including violent predators, to register as homeless or list a shelter or inexact location as long as they stay in touch with police." In making this comment, Koch proves that "Jessica's Law" has not made it much easier for parents to know where registered sex offenders live, considering the offender may be sleeping on the bench at the end of their street. Not only does the residency restrictions that "Jessica's Law" impose cause a large amount of registered sex offenders to become homeless, it also makes it extremely difficult for police officers to track them—which in turn, makes police lose faith in the effectiveness of the law. Palm Beach County Sheriff's Office Detective Larry Wood explained saying, "I don't believe they are working. They're assisting these guys in going underground" ("Critics Debate Effectiveness of Sex Offender Laws"). Police officers and politicians both know that this law was passed too quickly and did not have enough time to evolve into an effective law on safety. In fact, Corwin Ritchie, the executive director of the association of Iowa prosecutors, agrees, saying, "Most legislators know in their hearts that the law is no good and a waste of time . . . " (Associated Press "California's sex offenders beat tracking system"). The Jessica Lunsford Act not only makes it harder to track what registered sex offenders are doing, but offers a false sense of security to Americans, which can be just as harmful, if not more.

The second law, titled Megan's Law, has another safety complication that was over-looked. Megan's Law,—a law that was designed to set up online sex offender registries—is causing confusion among the public and often leading to innocent people being killed by vigilantes. Megan's Law was originally designed to require states to have some type of public registry consisting of sex offenders in the area, so that citizens could be aware of their surroundings. The problem with this act, unfortunately, is that all sex offenders and predators are lumped into one category. Bill Haben, an attorney and veteran Texas pardon and parole specialist said, "The registry now not only includes . . . youthful, consensual relationships—but others caught in the criminal justice web for things such as indecent exposure . . . which also includes the 'poor drunk' popped by police while urinating behind a 7-Eleven in the middle of the night" (Smith). Austin Police Department Lt. Greg Moss agrees explaining, "The public in general only hears, 'He's a registered sex offender.' Through ignorance, they believe that is synonymous with 'sexual predator'" (Smith). In other words, there is no way to tell if the neighbor down the street is a dangerous child molester or someone who made an innocent mistake in their teen years. There is no way to tell with the online registry Megan's Law set up. This law has also caused a rise in vigilantism against sex offenders and innocent bystanders. The Associated Press reported in February of 2009, "Timothy Chandler had been arrested on child pornography charges . . . Two of Chandler's neighbors decided to do something about it . . . They're accused of trying to scare him off by setting fire to his tiny house . . ." ("Vigilantes Torch Home, Kill Innocent Woman"). Charles Onley, a research associate for the Center for Sex Offender Management, said, ". . . critics of the online registries warned that readily available details about sex offenders could spur widespread vigilante-style killings" (Bazar). Having instantly accessible online information on registered sex offenders is not making this country any safer, it can often cause vigilantism against the families, or even someone one who looks like the offender. These acts of violence arise more often when a violent sexual abuse case engulfs the nation and citizens remember they have information readily available. In conclusion, Megan's Law not only confuses Americans on who is truly dangerous in their community but also provides the opportunity and resources for a new kind of violence.

Many people argue that the sex offender laws in America today, do indeed keep citizens safe. Parents and politicians say that the sex offender registries established with Megan's Law have provided a way to recognize the dangers that surround children and offer a source of protection. They also argue that the Jessica Lunsford Act keeps children safe when they are away from home, such as at school or the park. The online registries and residency restriction laws have many supporters, including Herbert Cohen, a lawyer for Mark Lunsford, saying, "If you limit these people that they can't be around where children play and go to school, that will take away the enticement" ("Critics Debate Effectiveness of Sex Offender Laws"). Essentially, he believes, like many others, that restricting sex offender's access to areas populated by children, will increase safety and lower crime. Connie Upshaw, a PTA member at Calusa Elementary School agreed, saying, "The bigger the feet, the better" ("Critics Debate Effectiveness of Sex Offender

Laws"). Most Americans believe that the laws politicians have put in place regarding sex offenders are effective and often, may not be extreme enough.

Although this argument has some merit, sex offender laws today are not making Americans safer. Residency restrictions do not directly effect where sex offenders can spend their days—essentially, predators could spend all day outside a school or park and plot their next crime. The California Sex Offender Management Board's new report to the state legislator reads, "There is almost no correlation between sex offenders living near restricted areas and where they commit their offenses" (Noyes). A perfect example of this, is the 2009 and 2010 cases of the rape and murder of Chelsea King and Amber Dubois. In 2009, Amber Dubois disappeared on her way to school and was never found ("Slain Teenager Amber Dubois Remembered"). In 2010, Chelsea King went missing after jogging in a park by her house (Fremd). Both were attacked, raped, and murdered by John Gardner III in a 10 mile radius of each other, one year apart, even though Gardner did not live nearby (Spagat "Chelsea King Case vs. Amber Dubois Case"). According to the online registries designed to keep children safe, he reported that he lived in Riverside, California with his grandmother, while really living with his mother in Escondido, California (Spagat, Thompson, and Wayland). The residency restrictions and online registries American's believe are making their children safer, tragically did nothing to save these two innocent girls. Dr. Richard Wright said it perfectly when he wrote in his book, ". . . government has a responsibility to enact laws that have the greatest chance of success" (5). Consequently, the American sex offender laws in place, such as Megan's Law and the Jessica Lunsford Act are not succeeding—these laws are not protecting children, they are not giving accurate information to parents, and they are not keeping sex offenders from committing new crimes.

In conclusion, laws meant to keep American citizens safe from registered sexual predators are failing at the very thing they were designed to do. Megan's Law and the Jessica Lunsford Act were inspired by two horrific crimes mourned by the nation. Despite the fact that these laws were constructed to protect the public, they have backfired by leading parents to falsely believe their children are safer then ever before. The laws have created a great amount of homeless offenders, causing police to loose track of them. Although I grant that monitoring dangerous sexual predators is needed to protect the American public and children, I still maintain that politicians did not format the laws appropriately and in turn, made Americans in more danger now than in the past.

Works Cited

"2009 Annual Report." *National Center for Missing and Exploited Children*. National Center for Missing and Exploited Children, 2011. Web. 28 June 2011. <http://www.missingkids.com/missingkids/servlet/ResourceServlet?LanguageCountry=en_US&PageId=3679>.

Associated Press. "California's sex offenders beat tracking system." *Msnbc.com*. Msnbc.com, 2011. 31 Oct. 2007. Web. 27 June 2011.

Associated Press. "Vigilantes Torch Home, Kill Innocent Woman." *CBSNEWS*. CBS Interactive Inc, 11 Feb. 2009. Web. 26 June 2011.

Bazar, Emily. "Suspected shooter found sex offenders' homes on website." *USA TODAY*. USA TODAY, 2011. Web. 27 June 2011.

"Critics Debate Effectiveness of Sex Offender Laws." *Sex Offender Issues*. Sex Offender Issues, 16 June 2007. Web. 27 June 2011.

Koch, Wendy. "Many sex offenders are often homeless." *USA TODAY*. USA TODAY, 18 Apr. 2006. Web. 27 June 2011.

"Megans Law, Registered Sex Offenders And Background Checks." *About . . . Megan's Law*. 2011. Web. 28 June 2011.

Noyes, Dan. "Jessica's Law dilemma: Homeless sex offenders." *ABC7*. ABC Inc, 28 Jan. 2011. Web. 28 June 2011.

"Slain Teenager Amber Dubois Remembered." *KTLA.com Los Angeles*. KTLA Inc, 27 Mar. 2010. Web. 27 June 2011.

Smith, Jordan. "Sex Offenders Exposed." *The Austin Chronicle*. Austin Chronicle Corp, 10 Sept. 2010. Web. 27 June 2011.

Spagat, Elliot. "Chelsea King Case vs. Amber Dubois Case." *myFOXla.com*. Fox Television Stations, Inc, 2011. Web. 28 June 2011.

Spagat, Elliot, Don Thompson and Michelle Wayland. "Why Gardner Eluded Suspicion." *NBC SAN DIEGO*. NBCUniversal Inc, 4 Mar. 2010. Web. 26 June 2011.

"The Jessica Lunsford Tragedy That Resulted In Jessica's Law." *About . . . Megan's Law*. 2011. Web. 28 June 2011.

Von Fremd, Mike, Sarah Netter and Russell Goldman. "Chelsea King Killing: Police Comb Grave for Clues." *Good Morning America*. ABC News Internet Ventures, 3 Mar. 2010. Web. 28 June 2011.

Waymire, Nathan. "Sex Offender Statistics." *Associated Content*. Yahoo! Inc, 30 Apr. 2010. Web. 27 June 2011.

Wright, Richard. *Sex Offender Laws*. New York: Springer Publishing Company, LLC, 2009. Print.

Name: _____

Questions

1. What is the author's main argument? What kind of claim is being made? Is this claim effective for this kind of essay? Explain.

_____

_____

_____

_____

2. Analyze one of the support paragraphs. What kind of support is being used? Is the support effective? Are there any support paragraphs that are not effective?

_____

_____

_____

_____

3. Discuss the introduction paragraph. Does the introduction hook the reader? Is the thesis clear and arguable? Explain.

_____

_____

_____

_____

4. Discuss some of the essay's strengths. What does it do well? Be specific.

5. Does the essay have any weaknesses? Explain. How can these weaknesses be improved?

6. Do you agree or disagree with the author? Why? Be specific by referencing the essay. This answer may be written in the form of your own essay.

Lorena Fernandez
June 13, 2011
English 68

Prison System Gets an F

America has the highest incarceration rate in the world. According to the Bureau of Justice Statistics, "1 out of every 142 Americans is now actually in prison" (Longley). Today, the purpose of putting criminals in prison is for punishment and/or rehabilitation. Putting criminals in prison does not mean that they are going to become better people and all the crime in the world is going to stop. Ex-convicts keep coming back to prison for committing crimes worse than before. The prison system in the United States has a negative effect on inmates. It is important to understand that these effects will make an inmate go back or stay longer in prison, which means the prison system is not working as it should.

The prison system is not rehabilitating the majority of inmates. The majority of inmates are leaving prison better criminals than they were when they first came to prison. When it comes to rehabilitating an inmate, the goal is to "reform the prisoners from committing crimes and assisting them in starting normal lives without any criminal activities" (Winkel). The prison system offers many programs like life skill classes, drug treatment, college, job training, and a variety of other programs. Some of these programs help the minority of inmates in prison, but they are not helping the majority of inmates. Many inmates are becoming better criminals in prison. For example, an offender is incarcerated for two years for a minor offense. He is thrown into a system where there are criminals who can teach this person how to do crimes "better." Therefore, the prison system has a high recidivism rate. Clare Hanrahan writes, "According to the Bureau of Justice Statistics, more than two-thirds of released prisoners are re-arrested within three years" (26). Many people believe that the prison system does rehabilitate many prisoners, but the recidivism rate shows that it does not. Many of the inmates that are trying to get rehabilitated from drugs do not, because they are able to obtain drugs from inside the prison.

Inmates are finding ways to get drugs delivered to them in prison. They can get them through visits from friends and relatives, mail, or by Correctional Officers. According to Crary, inmates are receiving drugs "via visiting relatives, by mail, through the complicity of prison staff, by inmates themselves who smuggle in drugs dropped off by associates at off-prison work sites". Five state correctional officers were accused of smuggling drugs inside Dade Correctional Institution, a maximum-security prison, in Florida. According to federal prosecutors, the officers "accepted cash payments from inmates in return for helping to deliver drugs inside the prison" ("Prison Guards Accused of Smuggling Drugs"). Correctional Officers are bringing in the drugs for inmates when they should be the ones trying to help the inmate be drug free. According to Gretl Plessinger, their ultimate goal is to get rid of drugs in prisons, but "I'd be a fool to tell you that will ever be realized" (Crary). Meaning, he would be stupid to say that they will get rid of drugs in prisons. Besides smuggling in drugs, another problem in the prison system is the smuggling of cell phones.

Drugs and weapons are not the only contraband in prisons today. Other items that they are finding in prisons are cell phones. Cell phones have become the most commonly traded object in prison. Inmates are getting a hold of cell phones and using them to communicate with people from inside and outside prison walls. In 2007, California Department of Corrections and Rehabilitation (CDCR) confiscated "1,400 cell phones from inmates" and in 2010 they "seized 10,000" ("CDCR Looking to Technology to Deter Contraband Cell Phones"). According to these statistics, it is becoming easier to bring cell phones inside prisons. According to legislative analysts, "prison employees, roughly half of whom are unionized guards, are the main source of smuggled phones that inmates use to run drugs and other crimes. Unlike visitors, staff can enter the facilities without passing through metal detectors" (Palta). In other words, prison employees, half of which are prison guards, are the main reason why cell phones are getting to inmates. Employees do no have to go through a metal detector like visitors do. Inmates are using cell phones to arrange crimes, call their family and friends, and even escape from prison. Richard Subia, assistant director for California's Division of Adult Institutions, said that a prisoner escaped from the prison and used a cell phone to get a ride out of town. The inmate called his girlfriend and told her to pick him up in a nearby town (McNichol). A reason why they have not stopped the smuggling of drugs in prisons is because many of the guards do not want to snitch on their co-workers selling phones to convicts. The guards turn their head and pretend they did not see anything. Some officers would try to solve the problem, but most of them just want to go to work, do their job, and go home safe. Since inmates are able to obtain drugs, cell phones, and many other things, prison is just like a home.

Prison should not be a place where inmates get to sleep all day and watch television. Prison is becoming like a "fun park" for many inmates. Many inmates commit crimes just so they can go back to prison. For most of them it is easier than being on the streets. They live in a place where a person does not have to do anything and he/she still has a room to sleep in, food to eat, and when they are sick, they will be able to get checked by a doctor at no cost. According to Isabelle Gonzalez, a current inmate at California Institution for Women, "when it is time for an inmate to parole, they hide because they do not want to leave prison. They do not want to go back and live in the streets or work." No wonder every year more ex-convicts want to go back to prison; everything they need is in prison. We are spending too much money to have criminals in prison just for them not to do anything. According to Sacramento, "Americans spend $60 billion a year to imprison 2.2 million people" (Warren). Also, their medical is fully covered by the state and they do not have to pay anything back. In 2010, the state of California spent an average of "$15, 296 per inmate" for healthcare (Warren). Those imprisoned for life should work long hours in the sun or in the cold repairing our highways or doing the tough jobs nobody else wants to do. Little by little they should pay back the money that the taxpayers pay for them. They acted out against society; they should pay the price of giving back to it. Inmates should not be sleeping and watching television all day.

The prison system in the United States is having no effect on prisoners. This is making inmates go back or stay longer in prison. Inmates are not being rehabilitated. They are coming out of prison better criminals than they were. Inmates are able to smuggle drugs inside the prison. They are obtaining drugs from staff, visiting, mail, and by other inmates. Another contraband inmates are getting a hold of is a cell phone. They are using it to plan escapes and plan crimes outside of prison. Prison is becoming easier than being in the streets. They have a room to sleep in, food to eat, and free health care. Prison can have a positive effect on inmates if only the system was stricter.

Works Cited

"CDCR Looking to Technology to Deter Contraband Cellphones." *Corrections Reporter.* The Corrections Reporter, 2011. Web. 2 June 2011.

Crary, David. "Prison Drug Use Becoming Harder and Harder to Control." CorrectionsOne.com. CorrectionsOne: The One Resource for Corrections, 2011. Web. 29 May 2011.

Gonzalez, Isabelle. Personal Interview. 1 June 2011.

Hanrahan, Clare. *America's Prisons.* Michigan: Greenhaven Press, 2006. Print.

Longley, Robert. "1 Out of 32 Americans Under Correctional Supervision. About.com. About.com, 2011. Web. 11 June 2011.

McNichol, Tom. "Prison Cell-Phone Use a Growing Problem." *Time.* Time Inc., 2011. Web. 26 May 2011.

Palta, Rina. "Why Cell Phones in Prisons Won't Go Away." *KALW News.* KALW. Web. 1 June 2011.

"Prison Guards Accused of Smuggling Drugs." *Local10.com.* WPLG, 2011. Web. 28 May 2011.

Warren, Jenifer. "High Cost of Prisons Not Paying Off, Report Finds." *CommonDreams.org.* CommonDreams.org, 2010. Web. 26 May 2011.

Winkel, Bethany. "Substance Abuse Among Inmates." *Treatment Solutions Network.* TreatmentSolutionsNetwork.com, 2011. Web. 28 May 2011.

Name: _____

Questions

1. What is the author's main argument? What kind of claim is being made? Is this claim effective for this kind of essay? Explain.

   _____

   _____

   _____

   _____

2. Analyze one of the support paragraphs. What kind of support is being used? Is the support effective? Are there any support paragraphs that are not effective?

   _____

   _____

   _____

   _____

3. Discuss the introduction paragraph. Does the introduction hook the reader? Is the thesis clear and arguable? Explain.

   _____

   _____

   _____

   _____

4. Discuss some of the essay's strengths. What does it do well? Be specific.

5. Does the essay have any weaknesses? Explain. How can these weaknesses be improved?

6. Do you agree or disagree with the author? Why? Be specific by referencing the essay. This answer may be written in the form of your own essay.

Chapter 5

Teen Suicide

Unfortunately, there are moments when teens feel they have nothing to live for and they commit suicide. There are many factors that can affect a teen, and therefore, alter the reason for the act of suicide. Clearly, teenage suicide deals with a wide range of causes and effects for everyone involved. In Priscilla Garcia's essay, she addresses some of the causes and effects of teenage suicide, and she argues that if we can understand more about this issue, we may be able to prevent teenage suicide in the future.

Priscilla Garcia
English 101
29 October 2009

Teenage Suicide

There are many teens who feel trapped in their lives, but what actually drives them to kill themselves? Imagine having a twelve year old child who has no one or nowhere to turn to, but to the face of death. How can anyone deal with such tragedy of losing a child to suicide? According to an online article, "Suicide is the third leading cause of death among adolescents and teenagers. According to the National Institute of Mental Health, about 8 out of every 100,000 teenagers committed suicide in 2000. For every teen suicide death, experts estimate there are 10 other teen suicide attempt" ("Teen Suicide Statistics"). Suicide is not only a major issue in America among adults, but also in teenagers. There are many different reasons for teenage suicide. The tragedy of suicide not only affects the teens committing suicide, but also the people around them. Understanding the different causes of teenage suicide is important because teen suicide is on the rise and can be prevented.

A major cause of teenage suicide is bullying. Bullying is when a person or group of people intentionally hurt a certain individual by physical and verbal abuse. Many teens are bullied at school or at home by friends or family members. Young bullying victims become scared of their tormentors, develop low self-esteem, and become isolated from the rest of society. In the article "Extreme Bullying Leads to Suicide," it reveals that, "A study by Yale University finds that bully victims are two to nine times more likely to report having suicidal thoughts than other kids." Bullying in teens is causing them to become suicidal. Recently, there have been more top news stories developing across America of young teens committing suicide due to bullying. For example, in an article from October 21, 2008, "Jeremiah Lassiter, a 15-year-old freshman, shot himself in the head in the school bathroom yesterday afternoon. He was a special-ed student who, according to students and school officials, was constantly bullied." ("Extreme Bullying Leads to Suicide"). This evidences how cruel teens are who bully the victim and hurt the victim so deeply that it can drive the victim to kill them self. In addition, bullying leads to depression which also leads to teens to kill themselves.

The leading cause of suicide among teens is due to several mental disorders. Among the several mental disorders that cause suicide, depression is the main disorder. Depression is triggered from problems at home, school, friends, family, or any other negative life experiences that have impacted their lives from verbal and/or physical abuse. Depression causes teens to feel lonely, despair, angry, humiliation, and extreme sadness. Some of these mental disorders can also be caused by different hormonal changes teenagers go through as they are transforming into young adults. According to the article, "Teen Suicide Statistics" it states that, "90 percent of teens who attempt or commit suicide suffer from a mental illness, such as: depression, bipolar disorder, and schizophrenia." In other words, teen suicide is mainly caused by mental disorders, with depression being the leading disorder. These disorders can be treated with medication and counseling to prevent suicide in teens, but first it needs to be diagnosed so friends, family, or loved ones can get teens the help they need. Consequently, teens dealing with depression and mental disorders are more likely to have drug abuse problems and result in suicide.

Another major cause of teen suicide is drug abuse. Drug abuse increases the feeling of depression, which can eventually lead teens to suicide. Drug abuse causes teen suicide because the drugs affect the ability of teens to be able to think clearly and enables them to focus on solutions to their problems. In the article "Teen Alcohol Use" the author writes, "When the "buzz" wears off, teenagers might feel even more depressed than they did before. These feelings can lead to suicidal thoughts, or even teen suicide attempts. Teens who realize they have a dependency can begin to feel hopeless as thought they will never escape their alcohol abuse. These feelings of hopelessness and increased depression can also lead to teen suicide." Teens need to realize that drug abuse is dangerous and unhealthy not only for their body, but especially for their mental health. Teen suicide is dangerous and always has negative consequences.

Teen suicide has a negative effect, which consequently leads to death of young adults and children. Teenagers committing suicide not only ultimately leads to the death of their own lives', but also it greatly affects the people around them that love and care for them. When people lose a teen or child because of suicide, it causes them to become sad and devastated. This sadness and devastation can also lead them into a deep depression and suicidal thoughts, which can also direct them to committing suicide as well. This means that the cycle of suicide starts all over again, starting with sadness, then deep depression, and finally suicide. It can become a pattern if the suicidal behaviors continue unnoticed. Teen suicide can be prevented with the proper diagnoses of the teen's depression, suicidal behavior, and analysis of their thoughts and feelings through counseling.

Teenage suicide needs to be more looked at by society in order to prevent this epidemic across America. Bullying among teens causes suicide more frequently in young teens that are victims of bullying than those who are not bullied. Teens and children experiencing extreme sadness, anger, low self-esteem, and loneliness result in depression. Depression along with other mental disorders can drive teenagers to commit suicide, which hurts the people around them who love and care for them. Teenage suicide in America is always a devastating tragedy and there should be severe consequences for those people who drive these innocent teens to kill themselves.

Works Cited

"Extreme Bullying Leads to Suicide." *Momlogic.com.* GNH Productions, Inc., 21 Oct. 2008. Web. 25 Oct. 2009. <www.momlogic.com/2008/10/jeremiah_lassiter_suicide _bull.php>.

"Teen Alcohol Use." *Teendepression.org.* 2005. Web. 26 Oct. 2009.

"Teen Suicide Statistics." *Teendepression.org.* 2005. Web. 26 Oct. 2009.

Name: _____

Questions

1. What is the author's main argument? What kind of claim is being made? Is this claim effective for this kind of essay? Explain.

_____

_____

_____

_____

2. Analyze one of the support paragraphs. What kind of support is being used? Is the support effective? Are there any support paragraphs that are not effective?

_____

_____

_____

_____

3. Discuss the introduction paragraph. Does the introduction hook the reader? Is the thesis clear and arguable? Explain.

_____

_____

_____

_____

4. Discuss some of the essay's strengths. What does it do well? Be specific.

_____

_____

_____

_____

_____

5. Does the essay have any weaknesses? Explain. How can these weaknesses be improved?

_____

_____

_____

_____

_____

6. Do you agree or disagree with the author? Why? Be specific by referencing the essay. This answer may be written in the form of your own essay.

_____

_____

_____

_____

_____

Chapter 6

Wal-Mart

Wal-Mart is one of the largest corporations in the world. With stores in multiple countries, Wal-Mart continually sees profits in the billions of dollars. The company's impact on all industries is unquestionable. However, is Wal-Mart a positive or negative force when it comes to the industries they affect? There are many arguments for and against Wal-Mart's actions. Rachel Roberts starts by explaining how employees are treated unfairly at Wal-Mart stores, resulting in lawsuits against the company. In Marlene Diaz's combo paragraph, she addresses the argument that Wal-Mart treats female and male employees differently. She uses the lawsuits (current and old) filed by women against the store as examples to prove her argument. However, Wal-Mart is not completely "evil," and Yadira Alicia Diaz shows that Wal-Mart is a positive corporation in the world.

Rachel Roberts
English 101
6-24-2011

The Rights of Workers at Wal-Mart

Many financial advisers and experts believe Wal-Mart is one of the best companies to ever influence the American job market. They believe Wal-Mart not only offers products at an extremely low price, but also more importantly, has provided great job opportunities to otherwise unemployable Americans. Wal-Mart employs roughly 1.4 million nationwide (Blodget). The Federal Reserve Bank of Minneapolis, who studied the "Wal-Mart Effect" for twenty years, found that, "personal income, overall employment and retail employment grew faster in counties with a Wal-Mart than in those without one" (Van Riper). Much of the public agrees that having a Wal-Mart in any populated area brings in more business and job prospects for the surrounding community. Howard Davidowitz, a retail analyst, stated in an interview, "Wal-Mart offers more opportunity than any company I've ever seen . . . They give you an opportunity. You don't need a fancy pedigree to go to work for Wal-Mart. . . . They are creating jobs. When they open a supercenter, thousands of people line up for jobs" (Curtin). Davidowitz celebrates the fact that Wal-Mart is generating more jobs, which are available to all Americans, in a time where careers are hard to come by because of high unemployment. The majority of Americans agree that the job market as of now is frightening and leaving a great deal of the public with no options—but that Wal-Mart continues to offer job opportunities all over the U.S., helping many Americans to continue feeding their families.

Although Wal-Mart creates a magnitude of jobs, I believe they are severely inconveniencing their employees by forcing most to live below the poverty line and struggle daily. The majority of Wal-Mart's employees go without health insurance and can barely afford to shop anywhere other than Wal-Mart. Greg Denier, the communications director for the United Food and Commercial Workers International Union, declared, "Americans can't live on a Wal-Mart paycheck" (Olson 344). The average Wal-Mart employee makes $20,744 a year, which is below the poverty level of $22,000 (Blodget). The essence of Denier's argument is to prove that Wal-Mart is not fairly compensating their workers and that managers need to raise the hourly wages of their employees. An anonymous overnight stocker from Minnesota, said, "We're unpaid, and I'm worried about my retirement. . . .I imagine I'll be working until I'm 90" (Olson 347). In fact, Wal-Mart has been known to underpay employees even from the beginning. When Sam Walton opened Wal-Mart in 1960, he "paid his first clerks 50 to 60 cents an hour—substantially below minimum wage at the time" (Olson 347). Taking into consideration that Wal-Mart's market value is $200 billion and they employ about 1% of Americans, Wal-Mart can surely afford to raise the hourly pay for employees and should do so willingly (Blodget). Wal-Mart would then set acceptable standards for wages and benefits while still make an extremely large profit. The fact that Wal-Mart, a company that makes millions of dollars every year, has employees living in poverty is despicable and needs to be changed.

Not only does Wal-Mart pay their employees the bare minimum, but managers over work them—sometimes even off the clock—resulting in many lawsuits from outraged employees. Wal-Mart under staffs and often asks employees to work hours after their shift is over without pay. Liberty Morales Serna, a former Wal-Mart employee, explained saying, "I was asked to work off the clock, sometimes by the store manager . . . They would know you'd clocked out already, and they'd say, 'Do me a favor. I don't have anyone coming in—could you stay here?' It would be like four or five hours. They were understaffed, and they expected you to work these hours" (Olson 349). Liberty's story demonstrates that Wal-Mart violated the wage-and-hour laws knowingly and needs to be held accountable. Fortunately, many employees at Wal-Mart are standing up for their rights, filing law suits, and are winning all over the U.S. Karen Olson, a writer for the *Washington Post*, wrote, "Workers in 27 states are suing Wal-Mart for violating wage-and-hours laws . . . an Oregon jury found the company guilty in December of systematically forcing employees to work overtime without pay" (344). She also writes, ". . . a former personnel manager named Carolyn Thiebes testified that supervisors . . . regularly deleted hours from time records and reprimanded employees who claimed overtime" (Olson 348). These two examples prove that Wal-Mart focuses more on making a profit than on the best interests of their employees. Although fair wages and work conditions at Wal-Mart may seem of concern to only a small percent of Americans, it should in fact concern anyone who cares about workplace integrity, making a comfortable living and keeping major corporations accountable, because Wal-Mart is the world's largest retailer and America's largest private employer—they set the standards for the rest. Bernie Hesse, an organizer for the UFCW, said it best, saying, "These are the jobs our kids are going to have" (Olson 354). In other words, today's generation of Americans need to stand up for what is right and insist that major corporations such as Wal-Mart, be held accountable for paying their employees fairly and providing workers with a safe and secure workplace, otherwise the next generation will be working for many different corrupt companies following Wal-Mart's example.

Works Cited

Blodget, Henry. "Walmart Employs 1% Of America. Should It Be Forced To Pay Its Employees More?" *Business Insider*. Business Insider, Inc, 2011. Web. 23 June 2011.

Curtin, Stacy. "HOWARD DAVIDOWITZ: Walmart Is Great For America—Unions Are Awful." *Business Insider*. Business Insider, Inc, 2011. Web. 23 June 2011.

Olsson, Karen. "Up Against Wal-Mart." *They Say, I Say with Readings*. Gerald Graff, Cathy Birkenstein and Russel Durst. New York: W.W. Norton & Company, Inc, 2009. 342–354. Print.

Van Riper, Tom. "Why Wal-Mart may just be good for the U.S." *Msnbc.com*. Msnbc.com, 2011. Web. 23 June 2011.

Name: _____

Questions

1. What is the author's main argument? What is the overall claim being made? Explain.

_____

_____

_____

_____

_____

2. Analyze one of the paragraphs. What kind of support is being used? Is the support effective?

_____

_____

_____

_____

_____

3. Discuss the flow of one of the paragraphs. Is the topic sentence effective? Does the rest of the paragraph match the topic sentence? Explain.

_____

_____

_____

_____

4. Discuss some of the strengths of this assignment. What does it do well? Be specific.

5. Does the assignment have any weaknesses? Explain. How can these weaknesses be improved?

6. Do you agree or disagree with the author? Why? Be specific by referencing the essay. This answer may be written in the form of your own essay.

Marlene Diaz
English 1C: 10:30
24 February 2012

Wal-Mart is for Boys, Not Girls

Many people argue that Wal-Mart discriminates against their women employees. Women employees at Wal-Mart are being paid less than men. According to a web article, it states "Wal-Mart has consistently paid their female employees less than their male counterparts . . . by an average of 22%" (Beachum). This article says that a woman employee is paid twenty-two percent less than a male employee. Moreover, another article states that women receive less pay "despite greater average seniority and higher performance ratings [and they are] being paid less even when they held the same jobs as men" ("Women of Wal-Mart Deserve their Day in Court: Retail Giant is *NOT* Too Big to Sue"). Women who work at Wal-Mart are getting unequal pay regardless of their status, and their wages are less than a male counterpart of the same standing. As a result, sexual discrimination seems embedded within Wal-Mart's foundations. Wal-Mart is discriminating women by paying them less than male workers.

It has also been argued that Wal-Mart does not promote women on a regular basis. There are more male managers than female managers. According to writer Karen Olsson, "more than two-thirds of all Wal-Mart employees are women-yet women make up less than 10 percent of top store managers" (350). Olsson states that women make up a significant amount of Wal-Mart workers, and yet there are a few who have been promoted to managers. In other words, women are not being promoted as much as men. In addition, National Organization for Women's (NOW) President Kim Gandy states "nationwide, two-thirds of the low paid 'sales associates' are women, while two-thirds of the management employees are men, and not surprisingly, 90% of the store managers are men as well." She states that women are constricted to the lowest paying jobs that Wal-Mart has to offer while a large portion of the male employees are located in the high paying positions. This implies that not only is Wal-Mart promoting fewer women to management jobs, it is keeping them in positions where they are getting less pay. A small amount of women employees are promoted in Wal-Mart and those who are not promoted are placed in the lowest paying jobs.

I agree that Wal-Mart discriminates against women by not promoting them to higher jobs. In fact, women have to struggle more in order to be promoted. In fact, according to "Women of Wal-Mart Deserve their Day in Court: Retail Giant is *NOT* Too Big to Sue," one of Wal-Mart's "shameful facts" is "women waiting longer for promotions" than men. This states that women have to endure a longer wait in order to be promoted. This results in not many women being promoted because they of that wait. Furthermore, another article written by Douglas Shuit gives a real instance where Edith Arana, a former Wal-Mart employee, went through various struggles in hopes of attaining a promotion:

> Keeping time records and maintaining personnel records for 200 employees was a lot of work, she says, but she was also asked to change the lights and close out cash registers when needed. She put up with the additional workload because she thought a management position was within her reach. Eventually, her ambitions were crushed and she was terminated in a dispute over time records . . .

This particular woman voluntarily does extra work, hoping that she will get one step closer to a promotion. Yet, she loses her chance and she is forced to witness her fellow male employees being promoted instead of her. Despite the fact that certain women work hard for a promotion, it seems as if men are promoted more easily than women. Wal-Mart does not make it simple for a woman to earn a promotion compared to men.

Works Cited

Beachum, Lateshia. "Wal-Mart's Employees Won't Benefit from New Slogan." *National Organization for Women*. National Organization for Women, 2012. Web. 24 Feb. 2012.

Gandy, Kim. "NOW Protests Wal-Mart Workplace Abuses." *National Organization for Women*. National Organization for Women, 2012. Web. 24 Feb. 2012.

Olsson, Karen. "Up Against Wal-Mart." *They Say, I Say: With Readings*. Ed. Gerald Graff, Cathy Birkenstein, and Russel Durst. New York: W.W. Norton & Company, 2009. 342–354. Print.

Shuit, Douglas P. "People Problems on Every Isle. (Cover Story)." *Workforce Management* 83.2 (2004): 26-34. *Academic Search Premier*. Web. 24 Feb. 2012.

"Women of Wal-Mart Deserve Their Day in Court: Retail Giant is *NOT* Too Big to Sue." *National Organization for Women*. National Organization for Women, 2012. Web. 24 Feb. 2012.

Name: _____

Questions

1. What is the author's main argument? What is the overall claim being made? Explain.

_____

_____

_____

_____

2. Analyze one of the paragraphs. What kind of support is being used? Is the support effective?

_____

_____

_____

_____

3. Discuss the flow of one of the paragraphs. Is the topic sentence effective? Does the rest of the paragraph match the topic sentence? Explain.

_____

_____

_____

_____

4. Discuss some of the strengths of this assignment. What does it do well? Be specific.

5. Does the assignment have any weaknesses? Explain. How can these weaknesses be improved?

6. Do you agree or disagree with the author? Why? Be specific by referencing the essay. This answer may be written in the form of your own essay.

Yadira Alicia Diaz
English 101
April 25, 2010

Wal-Mart: A Benefit to All

In today's world, people look for good quality items at a low price. Many people find great deals and shop at Wal-Mart. They choose to shop at Wal-Mart because it is convenient and inexpensive. Wal-Mart is today's best selling company because of their ability to provide low prices. Around the world today, there are over 7,000 Wal-Marts. Due to the fact that Wal-Mart is a large company, that makes them the largest employer. Wal-Mart also has a Foundation that contributes to several charities and helps people with disabilities. Wal-Mart also offers jobs to people with disabilities and seniors, unlike Target. Wal-Mart is important to our community because it is a large employer that offers low prices and makes it a possibility for people to survive. This is important because if Wal-Mart did not exist, there would be many people without work and struggling to feed their family. Furthermore, Wal-Mart benefit's people who are looking for low prices and jobs.

Wal-Mart offers jobs to people of all races, even with disabilities and regardless if their age is 57. Not many companies hire people with disabilities. For example, Target is a company that does not hire people with disabilities. One will not see seniors or people with disabilities at the front of a Target entry greeting and being paid to do it. According to an internet article in the *Los Angeles Times,* "Wal-Mart employs 2.1 Million workers in 8,000 stores world wide . . ." ("Court: Wal-Mart to face massive class action suit"). As a result of having thousands of stores, Wal-Mart has millions of employees working for them. In an internet article in *The Atlantic,* ". . . Wal-Mart is the nation's largest private employer" (McArdle). As one of the largest employers, Wal-Mart offers benefits such as medical and dental coverage. Wal-Mart also offers paid holidays, vacations and personal time to their employees. The employees have an opportunity to purchase stocks and participate in a 401K. According to Luzvie Fostanez, an employee at Wal-Mart, she says, "we receive 10% off regular price merchandise." In addition to benefits, employees are allowed to purchase items at an additional discount. Moreover, Wal-Mart is a good place for people to work and purchase there household items.

Wal-Mart offers low prices to everyone and makes it possible for people who are unemployed to survive. People enjoy finding items such as clothes, prescriptions and food at a reasonable price. People prefer to purchase their goods at Wal-Mart instead of Target. Wal-Mart is chosen by many people as their #1 store to shop because one can find everything. Wal-Mart's stores are convenient because they are open 24 hours. For example, if a person has an emergency and they need to pick up medicine or candles Wal-Mart will be open. People can pick up what they need in the middle of the night. In addition, Wal-Mart is one of the most successful companies in the world when it comes to sales because they are convenient and inexpensive. According to an internet article in

Fast Company, "Wal-Mart sold $244.5 billion worth of goods last year. It sells in three months what number-two retailer Home Depot sells in a year" (Fishman). This shows that Wal-Mart has low prices compared to others and sells more because they are reasonably priced. Due to their low priced items, Wal-Mart has been extremely successful in sales compared to Target and Home Depot. For example, Wal-Mart's sales have risen for 22 months in a row and Target's sales have fallen during that same time (Gregory). This shows that Wal-Mart has more customers than other stores. According to an internet article in *The New York Times*, ". . . as soon as products are on the shelves they begin to disappear into shopping carts" (Rosenbloom). People are constantly taking items off the shelves and the employees at Wal-Mart have to continuously stock. As a result, Wal-Mart has made a lot of money in sales and is able to give to people in need.

Aside from being a low priced store, Wal-Mart is a company that gives to those in need. The Wal-Mart Foundation donates to several charities, and helps communities around the world. According to an internet article in *PR Newswire*, "Wal-Mart Foundation today announced a $500,000 monetary donation to Red Cross relief efforts in Haiti. The company is also sending pre-packaged food kits valued at $100,000 to Haiti . . ." ("Wal-Mart $600,000 in Response to Haiti Earthquake"). Wal-Mart contributes money to people around the world and in our community. In an article in *The New York Times*, President and CEO of CARE, Helen Gayle, said "Walmart's support has made a significant difference in the lives of thousand of women, and their families, in Bangladesh, India and Peru" ("The Walmart Foundation to Increase Women's Development Partnership With CARE to a $3 Million"). The support of Wal-Mart has changed many lives around the world. This is occurring because Wal-Mart is giving them money and opportunities to change. According to *The New York Times*, "From Feb.1, 2009 through Jan. 31, 2010, Walmart and the Walmart Foundation gave more than $512 million in cash and in-kind gifts globally, $416 million of which was donated in the U.S" ("The Walmart Foundation to Increase Women's Development Partnership with CARE to $3 Million"). Wal-Mart has donated millions of dollars to people nation wide and worldwide. Furthermore, this is why Wal-Mart is making a difference all around the world.

Wal-Mart has made a difference not only to people in need, but has also been working on a digital program for medical providers. Wal-Mart is an extraordinary company that is trying to help people in the medical field become paperless. Having a paperless office will help our environment by saving trees and identity theft. According to an internet article in *The New York Times*, "Wal-Mart says its package deal of hardware, software, installation, maintenance and training will make the technology more accessible and affordable . . ." (Lohr). This has shown that Wal-Mart is also working on making technology affordable for everyone to have around the world where Wal-Mart's are located. Moreover, Wal-Mart is now targeting much more than shoppers at their stores, they will soon be working with the medical field equipment manufactures.

However, Wal-Mart is not as great as every one thinks, because they do not offer their employees the opportunity to be in a union. Wal-Mart is non-union and does not seem to be changing any time soon. For example, Wal-Mart does not provide benefits that union's offer such as low cost health coverage. Employees at Wal-Mart's do not have legal advice and support from a union that would help them if they would encounter a problem at work. They also do not have a union to fight for higher paying wages. Most unions provide pensions for their employees securing them with a better future when they retire. In an internet article in the *Boston.com*, ". . . Wal-Mart treats its employees and underscoring the company's extreme hostility to labor unions" (Johnson). Wal-Mart does not want to be associated with a union because they would loose certain power over their employees. There are many unions that would benefit employees at Wal-Mart such as the United Food and Commercial Workers International Union (UFCW). In the past, employees at Wal-Mart have tried to become a union, but have not been successful. According to an internet article in *Business Week,* "Nine days of negotiation between the UFCW and Wal-Mart produced nothing but acrimony" (Bianco). Wal-Mart has no intensions of becoming a union and only caused resentment to the employees. This has been occurring in different places around the world where Wal-Mart's are located. According to an internet article in *The Huffington Post*, "If Wal-Mart intends to nearly double its store count in Argentina over the next few years, it clearly needs to clean up its labor policies, and put on friendlier face towards organize labor" (Norman). In Argentina, the people there would like to see organized labor from Wal-Mart. In the United States, millions of workers would like to see higher wages and a better medical coverage. Furthermore, a union would be able to fight for those increases in benefits and help employees.

Nevertheless, people will continue to shop at Wal-Mart stores regardless if they are part of a union. This is because people do not care if the employees are getting the proper pay they deserve. People only care about the price they pay and the money that is being saved. A union would only cause prices to go up and that would not benefit people. As a result, one will have to pay higher prices for their items because Wal-Mart will have to pay higher wages if they became part of a union. In addition, unions are not ideal for people and shoppers because everyone will have to pay higher prices. Wal-Mart is a great store as it is and having a union would only cause fees to go up. People will not be able to afford to shop at Wal-Mart and this will cause starvation and poverty in our society.

On the other hand, Wal-Mart has often taken small business out of business and this occurs because they cannot compete with their low prices. Wal-Mart's low prices have caused small family owned businesses a lot of grief and sorrow. People cannot expect small businesses to be able to survive if Wal-Mart is offering the lowest prices that one can find. In an article in the *Los Angeles Times*, "The sharp cuts at its U.S Walmart stores, which came ahead of Memorial Day weekend, have already push rivals such as Target into price wars" (D'Innocenzio). This shows that Target has to lower their prices to be able to compete with Wal-Mart. As a result, Wal-Mart is often seen as a threat for small town stores because they are tremendously competitive. In an internet article, Richard Moe, The President of The National Trust for Historic Preservation said, "They tend to suck the economic life out of these downtowns, many which wither and die as a result" (Belluck).This is the outcome of Wal-Mart stores moving into towns where small stores cannot compete with their prices. People have seen Wal-Mart's move in and other small stores move out. According to Maria Esther Martinez, owner of a small store near a Wal-Mart, "When Wal-Mart opened their store, I stopped seeing some of my usual customers, I figured that they started shopping at Wal-Mart, business was not good so we stopped leasing our store." Maria unfortunately could not compete with Wal-Mart's low prices and as a result, she had to close her business. This is not unusual, but unfortunately, it happens to people in towns where Wal-Mart's are located. In addition, people will continue to see small business close or move because Wal-Mart is extremely competitive.

Regardless if small businesses are closing because of Wal-Mart's stores moving in, one will continue to shop at Wal-Mart. People often think that opening a Wal-Mart is not good for America, but when someone asked Hilary Clinton about Wal-Mart, she did not give a negative response. They asked her because she has been an important figure in today's society. In the book *The Retail Revolution*, ". . . Hilary Clinton, who had served six years on the Wal-Mart board . . ." said, "Well it's a mixed blessing . . ." (Lichtenstein 229). Hilary Clinton, was part of Wal-Mart's board of directors and thought of Wal-Mart as a mixed blessing. The reality is that Wal-Mart is good for people who are buying items and looking for good deals. People will always look for low prices and continue to shop there if prices do not change. When prices start to go up people will then look for other stores to shop, but as founder of Wal-Mart, Sam Walton said, "Always low prices." People will always be able to find their items at Wal-Mart because they will keep the prices as low as they can.

Wal-Mart will continue to be the #1 store because they have low priced items. People will continue to see Wal-Mart opening in many places around the world because they are convenient and useful to many. People should expect to see more Wal-Mart's because they are important to our economy. One will continue to see Wal-Mart's everywhere because they offer jobs and low priced items. Walt-Mart has gained from the community because of the uncountable contribution to people. It is clear that this company cares a lot for people regardless of the different ethnic background or physical disabilities. Walt-Mart embraced the community with great job opportunities that has made life much easier for many. At the same time, this great corporation strives to protect their employees by providing great benefits. Wal-Mart has demonstrated that they have the best prices and are extremely competitive. In the future people will continue to see more Wal-Mart's being open that are contributing jobs to those in need of employment.

Works Cited

Belluck, Pam. "Preservationists Call Vermont endangered by, Wal-Mart" *The New York Times.* The New York Times Com, 25 May 2004. Web. 16 May 2010.

Bianco, Anthony. "No Union Please, We're Wal-Mart." *Business Week.* Bloomberg L.P, 13 Feb. 2006. Web. 1 June 2010.

"Court: Wal-Mart to face massive class action suit." *Los Angeles Times.* Los Angeles Times, 27 Apr. 2010. Web. 4 May 2010.

D'Innocenzio, Anne. "Walmart bets on $1 ketchup, cheap soda, in campaign to re-ignite sales." *Los Angeles Times.* Los Angeles Times, 29 May 2010. Web. 31 May 2010.

Fishman, Charles. *The Wal-Mart Effect.* New York: Penguin Press, 2006. Print.

———. "The Wal-Mart You Don't Know." *Fast Company.* Mansueto Ventures LLC, 1 Dec. 2003. Web. 31 May 2010.

Fostanez, Luzvie. Personal Interview. 8 May 2010.

Gregory, Sean. "Walmart vs. Target: No Contest in the Recession." *Time.* Time Inc, 14 Mar. 2009. Web. 16 May 2010.

Johnson, Cecil. "A look inside the Wal-Mart business Model." *Boston.com.* The New York Times Com, 26 Feb. 2006. Web. 1 June 2010.

Lichtenstein, Nelson. *The Retail Revolution.* New York: Metropolitan Books, 2009. Print.

Lohr, Steve. "Wal-Mart Plans to Market Digital Health Records System." *The New York Times.* The New York Times Com, 10 Mar. 2009. Web. 1 June 2010.

Martinez, Maria Esther. Personal Interview. 9 May 2010.

McArdle, Megan. "Wal-Mart and Health Insurance: The Theories of the Case." *The Atlantic.* The Atlantic Monthly Group, 1 Jul. 2009. Web. 4 May 2010.

Norman, Al. "Buenos Aires Wal-Mart charged with Anti-Union Persecution." *The Huffington Post.* Huffpost Politics, 23 Jul. 2007. Web. 12 May 2010.

Rosenbloom, Stephanie. "My Initiation at Store 5476." *The New York Times.* The New York Times Com, 19 Dec. 2009. Web. 10 May 2010.

"The Walmart Foundation to Increase Women's Development Partnership with CARE to $3 Million." *The New York Times*. The New York Times Com, 10 May 2010. Web. 12 May 2010.

"Walmart Donates $600,000 in Response to Haiti Earthquake." *PR Newswire*. PR Newswire, Web. 8 May. 2010.

Name: _____

Questions

1. What is the author's main argument? What kind of claim is being made? Is this claim effective for this kind of essay? Explain.

   _____

   _____

   _____

   _____

2. Analyze one of the support paragraphs. What kind of support is being used? Is the support effective? Are there any support paragraphs that are not effective?

   _____

   _____

   _____

   _____

3. Discuss the introduction paragraph. Does the introduction hook the reader? Is the thesis clear and arguable? Explain.

   _____

   _____

   _____

   _____

4. Discuss some of the essay's strengths. What does it do well? Be specific.

_____

_____

_____

_____

_____

5. Does the essay have any weaknesses? Explain. How can these weaknesses be improved?

_____

_____

_____

_____

_____

6. Do you agree or disagree with the author? Why? Be specific by referencing the essay. This answer may be written in the form of your own essay.

_____

_____

_____

_____

Chapter 7

Economics and the Recession

This chapter covers a wide range of economic and social issues facing our country today. Since 2008, our country has been in a recession. The impact of that recession, and how to overcome it, is a source of countless political debates. The essays and assignments in this chapter deal with the smaller parts of the bigger issues, and they are not meant to be responses to each other. First, Wylie McGraw discusses the ability to reach the "American Dream." The concept of upward mobility has been part of this country a long time, but what happens if individuals are no longer to change their economic status? Yali Zhao examines America and its place in the world today and argues that what we stand for as a country is not over. Finally, Franchesca Cajigal examines the family unit and its affect on the country today. The recession has altered how families deal with each other, and the arguments about what this means and how to fix it play a role in our nation's recovery.

Wylie McGraw
English 101
27 June 2011

Economic Mobility

Today, many experts agree that the "American Dream" is on the verge of becoming extinct. In the 1960's the United States was virtually balanced as a middle-class country. Not as much can be said about how it looks and has been over the last 50 years. More so in the last decade has it been identified that only the top percentage of households have seen the overall gains while the average household has seen a loss in income, growing the poverty count in millions. Inequality is increasing vastly throughout the country. Americans are seeing the extreme separation of social groups based off economic status and that gap has developed the two distinct classes of people, the rich and the poor, where the rich are a concentrated minority and the poor that make up the rest. While the wealthy take on new tax cuts and larger profit margins, the lower income families must settle with little to no change with their income and huge budget cuts to their safety net that otherwise supports them where their wages cannot cover normal necessities. Holly Sklar, a policy analyst and syndicated columnist, author of "The Growing Gulf Between the Rich and the Rest of Us", a short essay in the book *They Say/I Say: with Readings*, touches on the content of the *Forbes 400*. She claims, "The United States has rising levels of poverty and inequality not found in other rich democracies . . . less mobility out of poverty" (308). Poverty, as well as inequality, takes a heavy toll everyday that is seldom seen through the media. She quotes from the 2005 Human Development Report, "The infant mortality rate in the United States compares with that in Malaysia—a country with a quarter the income and infant death rates are higher for [black] children in Washington, D.C., than for children in Kerala, India" (Sklar 309). These stunning facts give the reader an idea of the substantial irregularities and inequalities Americans are facing. They depict briefly how capitalism is slowly destroying the once fair and attainable financial security that all strive for here within the United States. The rich get richer, the middle class become the poor, and according to the *Census Bureau's* latest count, 37 million Americans are said to be below the poverty line. In other words, without change, the gap between the rich and the rest will continue to grow, weakening the U.S. economy and its democracy.

Other experts are also talking about the high and rising inequalities in the country and its effects on living standards. Researchers have shown over the last thirty years the larger share of economic growth has made its way to a small, wealthy minority, and the average family has seemed to lack the benefit technological progress brings. This lack of progress for the majority of families, who are at the lower and middle income brackets, is an important reason for many to seek the equal distribution of wages. Not only does inequality in this perspective damage the livelihood of American citizens, it brings about huge issues with society and democracy. A professor in economics at *Princeton* and writer for the *New York Times*, Paul Krugman writes about confronting inequality in an essay established in the book, *They Say/I Say: with Readings*, and mentions, "Ever since America's founding, our idea of ourselves has been that of a nation without sharp class distinctions—not a level society of perfect equality, but one in which the gap between the economic elite and the typical citizen isn't an unbridgeable chasm" (323). So what happened to the way Americans view and treat one another? It seems that greed has played a major role in the drastic change in society over the past generation. Social inequality is brought out by the vast income inequality currently consuming the American economy and it has negative consequences for the way citizens live here in America. Millions buy homes they truly cannot afford, acquiring mortgages and debt they will not be able to handle safely. This is the case when people are desperate to give their children a good education and put them in quality schools. He writes, ". . . An intensifying inequality means that the desirable school districts are growing fewer in number and more expensive to live in" (Krugman 325). He also goes on to say, "What it all comes down to is that although the principle of 'equality of opportunity, not equality of results' sounds fine, it's a largely fictitious distinction. A society with highly unequal results is . . . a society with highly unequal opportunity, too" (Krugman 328). It is a sad day that many Americans are caught up in this reality when all they are looking for is to give their children a chance in today's unequal society. To put in perspective, Krugman states, "A bad start can ruin a child's chances for life" (326). People can argue that you make your own way here in America and no matter how it is argued; the facts about inequality seem to state otherwise.

American social inequality has become a distinct problem as the economic growth has made the rich richer, but has not made its way down to the rest of Americans. The real question here is: Who is to blame for this ongoing crisis? It seems that the middle-class has been taking the heat of the national debt and in the wake of this, budget cuts for their health care, education, and the programs designed to help assist the families of lower income groups who cannot afford necessities based off their wages. It seems unfair that the wealthy receive tax breaks and not has to worry that their incomes will do anything but go up. Republicans can easily be blamed for their willingness to cut social programs from job training to health care. Doing so will worsen the income inequality. What makes this much more painful is the notion that America is the place where people can have a good life when they put in the hard work and abide by the rules. In the short story, "Inequality and the American Dream," also found in *They Say/I Say: with Readings,* a London-based weekly publication called *The Economist* states, "America defines itself by a collective dream: the dream of economic opportunity and upward mobility." Therefore, it makes sense that the United States is the most desired place of migration for people from all over the world. The publication, in response to this ideal, asks the question, "Who cares if the boss earns 300 times more than the average working stiff. If the stiff knows he can become the boss" (316)? So why, with the supremacy of the U.S. capitalistic economy, do most Americans believe that the economy is in bad shape? With George Bush's boast that the "the economy is powerful, productive, and prosperous," the vague middle class seems to feel the most pressure as the average worker's wages drift slowly while big corporate entities see massive profit margins. According to The Economist, "A college degree is no longer a passport to even higher pay" (317). There are insurmountable issues at hand with America and its dynamism, issues that take away from the merit of the country and shake up the logic of non-Americans, logic that "if globalization makes their economy like America's, and the American model is defective, then free-trade and open markets must be bad" (The Economist 318). America is known for not taking care of its poor. This was highly displayed by the events following Hurricane Katrina. Inequality has come in more of a complex way that it may appear. The rich are leaving the rest of the population behind while the middle-class loses its jobs to outsourcing and the bottom tier (the poor) are worried about immigration of rival workers being sponsored by Americans, even though there is no real proof that this is causing the lowering of current wages. This forum exclaims in disagreement, "Inequality is not inherently wrong-as long as three conditions are met first: society . . . getting richer, second, there is a safety net for the very poor, and third, everybody . . . has an opportunity to climb up through the system" (The Economist 319). Unfortunately, it seems as if it is easier for poorer children to make headway in most European countries than in they would in the United States. The question that is raised is what must be done? When there is no fairness, how can meritocracy prosper? Education is suffering the most and politicians are spending too much time trying to bring down the rich instead of helping others climb the social ladder. Another key point in the newspaper is the report that "education is a political football, tossed between Republicans who refuse to reform . . . and Democrats who will never dare offend their paymasters in the teachers unions" (The Economist 320). Health care, taxes, public pension, all social-welfare, need reform badly. Although America is still leading the rest of the world in how it can be done, the overall economy needs a serious overhaul. Without a new birth of idealism, the dynamic could change and the United States will ultimately lose its global merit.

Works Cited

Krugman, Paul. "Confronting Inequality." *They Say/I Say: with Readings*. Gerald Graff, Kathy Birkenstein, & Russell Durst. New York. W.W. Norton & Company, 2009: 322–341. Print.

Sklar, Holly. "The Growing Gulf Between the Rich and the Rest of Us." *They Say/I Say: with Readings*. Gerald Graff, Kathy Birkenstein, & Russell Durst. New York. W.W. Norton & Company, 2009: 308–311. Print.

The Economist. "Inequality and the American Dream." *They Say/I Say: with Readings*. Gerald Graff, Kathy Birkenstein, & Russell Durst. New York. W.W. Norton & Company, 2009: 316–321. Print.

Name: _____

Questions

1. What is the author's main argument? What is the overall claim being made? Explain.

_____

_____

_____

_____

_____

2. Analyze one of the paragraphs. What kind of support is being used? Is the support effective?

_____

_____

_____

_____

_____

3. Discuss the flow of one of the paragraphs. Is the topic sentence effective? Does the rest of the paragraph match the topic sentence? Explain.

_____

_____

_____

_____

_____

4. Discuss some of the strengths of this assignment. What does it do well? Be specific.

5. Does the assignment have any weaknesses? Explain. How can these weaknesses be improved?

6. Do you agree or disagree with the author? Why? Be specific by referencing the essay. This answer may be written in the form of your own essay.

Yali Zhao
English 1C
27 January 2010

America Today

As multiple nations with potentially more economic and technological growth than the United States emerged, the fear is that now America is now not just falling behind, but failing as a whole. Just by reading a newspaper published within the last five years, an example being the *Washington Post*, one can clearly see the sentiment that "U.S. influence is in steep decline" (Dowd 404). However, Alan W. Dowd, editor of *World Politics Review*, argues that this is not so in his article "The Decline and Fall of Declinism" published an issue of *the American*. The economy, for example, is the number one factor Americans point out as being greatly challenged, but Dowd points out that the US economy still represents 20% of global output, and is growing faster than 25 economies of the EU combined (Dowd 405). If anything, this proves that the American economy is still a force to be reckoned with internationally. China, the country seem as the most threatening to America's omnipotent position in the world market, only has a per capita income of roughly $2,069 compared to America's $44,244 (Dowd 406). Even though the cost of living in China is far cheaper than living in America, each American still makes roughly 20 times more than the average Chinese, not to mention that the standard of living in America is also far higher than in China. All together, the data seems to point to the fact that America has not lost its influence in the world economy.

While international renown is indeed useful politically, it still does not matter to the average American whether or not the nation's position in the world is unrivaled. The trouble with the great American Dream is that with it comes the great American ego, and as a comparatively young country that achieved the position of power after World War II, Americans have become much too comfortable to being in the number one position in the world. Then the rest of the world began to rise, America's first thought was not one of global equality, but fear that there are potential challengers to our position as the world's last superpower. However, just because the world is now doing much better does not directly mean that America's influence is now ending, rather that the world is now becoming more equal. Instead, America should be focusing on improving the lives of its people rather than trying to compare itself to the rest of the nations in the world.

Even when one turns its attention to within America, the numbers are still quite impressive. For one thing, although the majority sentiment is that America spent far too much on defense programs, the defense budget is still only about 4 percent of US GDP (Dowd 407). This still leaves a huge amount to be allotted to everything else, which also explains why America can endure so many crippling instances over the past few years that would have severely ruined any other country. 9/11, for instance, cost America an estimated $500 billion dollars in GDP, about half of the Canadian economy, and Hurricane Katrina cost the government $122 billion just in the year following the storm

(Dowd 407). While this amount would have been devastating to any other nation, America was able to gather up enough resources at the last minute and still did not affect the economy as a whole. If this is not proof that America was still going strong, than nothing will convince Americans at all.

While America may not be able to claim first place in all categories in the future anymore, it does not mean that America is in any way over, as the current headlines seem to suggest. The logical conclusion to be reached is simply that the world is now doing much better as a whole, and from an altruistic perspective this is something that should be celebrated. What the United States can offer is the high standard of living and the freedom that many other countries cannot. However, the media seems to be more focused on the numbers that prove nothing about the quality of life within America. The government's main concern should not be on some arbitrary numerical data that most likely would not affect its citizens at all. Rather than increasing the sales of the big companies in hopes that the wealth will trickle down to the middle and lower classes, it is much better to focus on improving the lives of the lower classes so they have the means to contribute more to the economy. Clinging on to the superpower status and trying to best everyone else will accomplish nothing but inflate the American ego, and would only lead to outrage both internally and internationally in the long term. As a nation, America's greatness does not depend on whether or not the nation is still standing on top of the world, and that America needs to learn to be content with what they can contribute to the world market, which is, at the moment, still quite significant.

Works Cited

Dowd, Alan W. "The Decline and Fall of Declinism." *They Say, I Say: With Readings.* Ed. Gerald Graff, Cathy Birkenstein, and Russel Durst. New York: Norton and Company, 2009. 172–180. Print.

Name: _____

Questions

1. What is the author's main argument? What is the overall claim being made? Explain.

   _____

   _____

   _____

   _____

   _____

2. Analyze one of the paragraphs. What kind of support is being used? Is the support effective?

   _____

   _____

   _____

   _____

   _____

3. Discuss the flow of one of the paragraphs. Is the topic sentence effective? Does the rest of the paragraph match the topic sentence? Explain.

   _____

   _____

   _____

   _____

4. Discuss some of the strengths of this assignment. What does it do well? Be specific.

5. Does the assignment have any weaknesses? Explain. How can these weaknesses be improved?

6. Do you agree or disagree with the author? Why? Be specific by referencing the essay. This answer may be written in the form of your own essay.

Franchesca Cajigal
English 101
06-30-11

The American Family

According to a 2010 poll of parents of children between the ages of 6 and 16 conducted by American Express, 71% of respondents said their children understand that the economy is in a recession ("Children Clued in to the Recession and Family Finances"). This astonishing number of aware children shows that family finances affect even the youngest family members. Many parents are sharing their current economic situations with their children. These dialogues between parents and children are just one example of how American families are reacting to their new economic position. The current recession (now named the Great Recession by most media outlets) has lasted from December 2007–June 2009 ("US Business Cycle Expansions and Contractions"). The Rockefeller Institute found that 20% of Americans have had their household income decreased by 25% or more since the recession started (Warner). With the reduction of family incomes so apparent across this nation, no family should have to feel that they are the only ones making sacrifices. Even though the recession is "officially" over, many American families are still feeling its economic affects. American families are adjusting and changing for the better in the wake of the recession. Family roles and responsibilities are being looked at in new ways as families stay together as times get tough economically in America.

Business researchers agree that employees today are putting their families before their work. In the wake of massive layoffs and company closures, Americans are realizing that years of putting the company first before their families has not paid off. According to a recent survey by the Florida State University College of Business, 48% of full-time employees surveyed felt an increased appreciation for their family since the recession. Researcher Tyler Everett explains, "Many of the people that we talked to felt that having less faith in work afforded them opportunities to direct more faith toward other often-neglected areas of life, and in most cases, it was family and friends" (Potvin). For many Americans losing their jobs or taking demotions or pay cuts put their work ethics into a new perspective. Many parents have to make hard choices between family and work. Often working parents have to miss school, sports, or social events their children participated in order to get ahead at work. Now, as many Americans have lost their faith in their jobs, they are now beginning to realize what opportunities they may have missed with their families.

As economic times became more difficult, American families started to pull together to make the most out of their new economic situations. In some families, complete parental role reversals were necessary. Many of the jobs lost since the recession has been in male dominated industries such as manufacturing and construction. In just these two examples, there have been 2 million layoffs (Hanes). With their husbands out of work, many wives have now become the main source of income for the family. Their husbands have now assumed the role of caregiver to their children, saving money on unneeded day care costs. This added time at home has helped countless fathers reconnect with their children. Many fathers welcome this change at first, but according to one stay at home dad interviewed, "What woman will say she doesn't want a guy who is home every night and cooks every meal and does all the shopping? But eventually it becomes self-emasculating. People wonder, 'Where's the man?'" (Hanes). Role reversal is hard on the masculine self-image. Even though Americans are more accepting of female wage earners, it is still not viewed as the norm. A Family and Work Institute study found that 41% of workers still believe in the traditional role of the husband bringing home the money while the wife looks after the children (Hanes). Although times are changing in America, many Americans still hold to traditional values. These values have shaped our ideals about how families should be. However, the reality today is American families are changing to what they need to be in order for their families to survive.

It is important for Americans to foster family togetherness during these tough economic times. Americans should be supportive of families who have had to make tough decisions in order to keep their families together. Many Americans are looking back to simpler times as they seek solutions in the future. This is described by *New York Times* writer Judith Warner as, "A craving for a simpler, slower, more centered life, one less consumed by the soul-emptying crush of getting, and spending, runs deep in within our culture right now." America had been running full force in economic growth prior to the recession. Now American families have had to come to a halt, and reassess what is important to them. Families prior to the recession had discretionary income to spend on luxury SUVs and extended vacations. Now, American families are discovering that less money affords them more free time for family and volunteering. Warner's belief is that people are doing more for their community and for each other. More and more Americans are reaching out to each other and supporting those who have less than they do. The era of consumerism has temporarily paused for America as Americans are fulfilled by helping others instead of themselves.

Parents want to provide a nice home for their children to grow up in. Many families prior to the recession were able to provide these homes for their children on their own. Now, after much job loss, many of these families have seen their homes taken away from them. Whether they lost their home in a foreclosure, or they simple just cannot afford the rent any longer, many unemployed parents are without a home for their families. The solution many of these parents are finding laid in their own childhood homes. Many grown children with families are moving back in with their parents in order to save money and place a roof over their children's heads. Census Bureau data shows that multifamily households have grown 11.7% from 2008 to 2010. This is the highest number of multifamily households since 1968 (Luo). Deciding to become a multifamily unit is a hard decision many families have had to make. The sharing of housing costs and bills is necessary for many of these families to survive. There are other advantages for some families. Many families experience more family time, allowing grandparents to watch closely their grandchildren growing up. However, there are also many disadvantages such as grandparents intruding on parenting responsibilities, individual family time alone, intimacy for parents, and different views of household responsibilities (Luo). Many families who decide to combine have done so as the last possible solution. Many grown children with their own families do not want to move back home with their parents, but do so out of necessity.

Family planning clinics are experiencing more requests for their services now than before the recession. Many families are putting off growing their family because they simply can not afford to raise a child. Planned Parenthood clinics in St. Petersburg and Sarasota had a 14% increase in abortions in the beginning of 2009 compared to the same period the year before (Anton). Women are being forced to make a hard choice between affording to have a child or having the pregnancy terminated. The rises in the abortion rates show that for many women the choice is an economic one. Men are also doing their part to keep the family unit from growing. Many more doctors are performing vasectomies. With a failure rate of less than 1%, men have control over this effective birth control (Hagen 143). Pinellas County Florida reported that the county paid for 305 vasectomies in 2008, up from 195 in 2006. In addition, in just the first six months of 2009 already the county paid for 193 vasectomies (Anton). The rise in vasectomies shows that men are thinking ahead about the size of their families. The recession is touching families more than in their pocketbook, it is also changing how big they would have become.

Many married couples who were considering divorce prior to the recession, decided put aside their divorce plans. According to the National Marriage Project ran by the University of Virginia, 38% of married couples surveyed who were considering divorce or separation prior to the recession changed their minds. Of these couples who decided to recommit to their marriage because of the recession, "52% reported to be much more likely to be in a happy marriage" (Wilcox). Couples today are reconnecting and discovering that they can get through difficult times together. Some experts cite that couples cannot afford to divorce and decrease their incomes. Whatever the factors are, it is apparent that the divorce rate in America is declining. In fact, the divorce rate has been waning since the early 1980's (Watson). Couples are staying together. Not only are couples not divorcing, they are not cheating on each other either. According to Bradford Wilcox, PhD., a sociologist and director of the Marriage and Family Project at the University of Virginia, "Infidelity has come down modestly since the 1990s. Americans are more likely now to express disapproval of infidelity than they were in the 1970s" (Watson). There seems to be a growing stigmatism towards divorce and infidelity in America. Adults, who grew up in the wake of the 1980's divorce boom, have decided that the path of divorce is not the road for them. More and more couples are working through difficult times and are staying together for themselves and their families.

The recession has made Americans change the way they live and think. Americans are now appreciating their families more and working less. Fathers are staying home and raising their children as their wives go to work to earn a living. Families are spending their money on what their family needs, not what their family wants. Grown children are returning to their parents homes with their own children in tow. Many Americans are deciding not to have more children. Moreover, contrary to what many people believe, Americans value their marriages and are choosing to stay together. Yes, the American family has changed immeasurably since the rescission. This change has been for the better, the American family is strong again.

Works Cited

Anton, Leonora LaPeter. "Recession affects family planning, with abortions and vasectomies up." *St. Petersburg Times*. St. Petersburg Times, 29 Mar. 2009. Web. 20 June 2011.

"Children Clued In To Recession and Family Finances." *American Express*, 2011. Web. 26 June 2011.

Hagen, Philip. *Mayo Clinic: Guide to Self-Care 4th ed.* Minnesota: Mayo Clinic Health Information, 2003. 143. Print.

Hanes, Stephanie. "How the recession is reshaping the American family." *The Christian Science Monitor*. The Christian Science Monitor, 14 June 2009. Web. 21 June 2011.

Luo, Michael. "Doubling Up' in Recession-Strained Quarters." *The New York Times*. The New York Times Company, 28 Dec. 2010. Web. 22 June 2011.

Potvin, Lindsay. "Americans rethinking role of work amid painful recession, says COB researcher." *Florida State University*. Florida State University, 18 Oct. 2010. Web. 20 June 2011.

Warner, Judith. "What the Great Recession Has Done to Family Life." *The New York Times*. The New York Times Company, 06 Aug. 2010. Web. 26 June 2011.

Watson, Rita. "Valentine love soars, infidelity dips." *The Seattle Times*. The Seattle Times Company, 10 Feb. 2011. Web. 27 June 2011.

Wilcox, Bradford. "The Great Recession and Marriage." *The National Marriage Project: University of Virginia*, 2011. Web. 24 June 2011.

"US Business Cycle Expansions and Contractions." *National Bureau of Economic Research*. National Bureau of Economic Research, 2010. Web. 23 June 2011.

Name: _____

Questions

1. What is the author's main argument? What kind of claim is being made? Is this claim effective for this kind of essay? Explain.

_____

_____

_____

_____

2. Analyze one of the support paragraphs. What kind of support is being used? Is the support effective? Are there any support paragraphs that are not effective?

_____

_____

_____

_____

3. Discuss the introduction paragraph. Does the introduction hook the reader? Is the thesis clear and arguable? Explain.

_____

_____

_____

_____

4. Discuss some of the essay's strengths. What does it do well? Be specific.

5. Does the essay have any weaknesses? Explain. How can these weaknesses be improved?

6. Do you agree or disagree with the author? Why? Be specific by referencing the essay. This answer may be written in the form of your own essay.

Chapter 8

Gun Control

You may have heard the expression, "Guns don't kill people, people kill people." Gun control laws are a serious issue in this country, and they greatly affect politics and the debate about safety. This idea goes back to the constitution and the "right to bear arms." Today, what does this mean? What rights should we have, and if guns are regulated, how should this be done? First, Jeffrey Hunt argues that gun control laws and the restrictions placed on citizens make it easier for criminals to obtain and use guns, and that studies show an increase in crime as these laws tighten their grip. On the other hand, Lam Nguyen argues in his essay that gun laws should be increased and strictly enforced in order to create a safer society. Two different views, two different arguments—what do you believe?

Jeffrey Hunt
English 68
5/25/2011

Gun Control Laws Fail

Due to the impossibility of tracking private transactions, guns can be acquired by anyone who truly desires them. Should laws come into effect which restrict or prohibit the trade of guns, they will instead be sold on the black market. The UK is a nation with strict gun control laws and is a vocal proponent of gun control policies. However, British intelligence experts estimated the presence of four million illegal guns in the country during 2005 (Goodchild). The estimated population of the UK for 2010 by the Office for National Statistics was 61.8 million ("Population Estimates: UK population grows to 61.8 million."). Assuming there was no significant change in the population of the UK over the course of six years, those numbers calculate to approximately one illegal weapon for every fifteen and a half citizens, or 6.47% of the population. Most of these weapons would have found their way into the country through smuggling, but many were also conversions of gun replicas that were only designed to fire blank rounds, meaning that firearms are also crafted within the country (Goodchild). Weapons will find their way into the hands of people that want them the most, the ones who are willing to break the law to acquire them.

Laws controlling or prohibiting the trade of firearms will be ineffective at preventing gun-related crimes due to the fact that the only individuals who would have free access to guns are the ones who are not above breaking the law to acquire them. Law abiding citizens without legal access to firearms are left with very few means to defend themselves against armed criminals. Because criminals will not have to worry about engaging with a person that is armed, crimes can be committed with greater frequency. Exemplifying this principle is the correlation between the UK gun ban and gun-related crime rates in that country. Over a period of two years following the introduction of the British handgun ban, an initial study from the Centre for Defence Studies reported that the number of gun-related crimes in 1999/2000 was about 3,685, a change of about 39% over the 2,648 in 1997/1998. ("Handgun crime 'up' despite ban"). Additionally, the British government reported that gun-related crimes had risen from 5,209 in 1998/1999 to 9,865 in 2008/2009, an alarmingly high 89% increase (Slack). Though many factors can influence crime rates, the likelihood of the correlation between the gun ban and the rise in gun-related crime rates actually being a causal relationship is very high; very few other factors are more relevant and could conceivably cause such a great change in gun-related crime rates. Without the availability of firearms to citizens, criminals are not deterred by the possibility of resistance and are free to more safely perform crimes.

With as often as firearms are favored by criminals and are criminalized in themselves, lawbreakers are more intimidated by the possibility of being shot by a potential victim. In 1982, a study concerning criminals and the role of guns was conducted upon 1,874 imprisoned felons ("The Armed Criminal In America"). It was found that 74% of criminals chose to avoid home invasion while the homeowner was present, for fear of being shot. Further study revealed that 34% of the interviewed prisoners admitted to engaging their victim, only to discover they were carrying a gun, and a very close figure of 37% admitted to being "scared off, shot at, wounded, or captured by an armed citizen" ("The Armed Criminal In America"). With three quarters of would-be home invaders turning away at the suspicion of encountering a gun-wielding homeowner, and over a third of other felons, who survived their encounter, being deterred by a gun in other crimes, the benefits of gun ownership become apparent. Most would-be criminals are discouraged from acting out in a society where gun ownership is the norm.

Works Cited

Goodchild, Sophie and Paul Lashmar. "Up to 4m guns in UK and police are losing the battle." *The Independent.* independent.co.uk, 4 Sept. 2005. Web. 25 May 2011.

"Handgun crime 'up' despite ban." *BBC News.* BBC, 16 July 2001. Web. 25 May 2011.

"Population Estimates: UK population grows to 61.8 million." *Office for National Statistics.* Office for National Statistics, 24 June 2010. Web. 25 May 2011.

Slack, James. "Culture of violence: Gun crime goes up by 89% in a decade." *MailOnline.* Associated Newspapers Ltd, 27 October 2009. Web. 25 May 2011.

"The Armed Criminal In America." *National Rifle Association Institute for Legislative Action.* National Rifle Association of America, Institute for Legislative Action, 9 Sept. 2003. Web. 25 May 2011.

Name: _____

Questions

1. What is the author's main argument? What is the overall claim being made? Explain.

   _____

   _____

   _____

   _____

2. Analyze one of the paragraphs. What kind of support is being used? Is the support effective?

   _____

   _____

   _____

   _____

3. Discuss the flow of one of the paragraphs. Is the topic sentence effective? Does the rest of the paragraph match the topic sentence? Explain.

   _____

   _____

   _____

   _____

4. Discuss some of the strengths of this assignment. What does it do well? Be specific.

5. Does the assignment have any weaknesses? Explain. How can these weaknesses be improved?

6. Do you agree or disagree with the author? Why? Be specific by referencing the essay. This answer may be written in the form of your own essay.

Lam Nguyen
English 101
11-7-10

Wanted: Gun Control Laws

In 2008, the FBI reported there were roughly 16,272 murders committed in the United States. Of these, about 10,886 or 67% were committed with firearms ("2008 Report: Crime in the United States, Expanded Homicide Data"). Today, despite the fact that a large number of people are murdered by guns; the usage of them is still becoming more popular in the United States. With this many lives being lost, it really makes people wonder whether the gun control laws need to be stricter. Since using firearms has both positive and negative effects, gun control has become a controversial issue for years. For every reason each side has, the opposing side will find an equal but opposite point for that belief. While some people believe that strictly enforcing the laws of gun control would quickly reduce the threat of crime, others say that guns protect their lives and it is their rights to possess and carry guns. The second amendment of the United States Constitution states that people have the right to keep and use firearms for self-defense against criminals. However, when people are able to carry guns with them and guns are kept at home or sold in public stores, the purpose of using firearms is not as simple as for people's protection. Therefore, the use of firearms should be strictly limited to eschew guns from criminals. Guns are made mostly to kill people and the possession of firearms has increased the rate of homicide in the United States. Understanding the arguments of anti-gun supporters will help people understand why gun regulation is needed in order to make life more peaceful.

One of the most common reasons that make American people buy guns is for self-defense. Under the laws of the Constitution, people have the right to own guns to defend themselves from criminals as well as the threat of tyranny. Unfortunately, buying a gun for this purpose usually ends up hurting the very people who were supposed to be defended by it. The reason is not everyone knows how to operate guns properly or can stay calm while facing criminals. Getting firearms for self-defense is also a major argument of the debate over gun control. However, according to Francis Hoey's statistics, using guns for self-defense is often ineffective, and people who use guns to defend themselves are 8 times more likely to be killed than those who do not (79). In essence, the chance of success when using firearms to defend against criminals is very low. This happens because the victims, who are the innocent people, rarely or never use firearms so they are not familiar with guns, or they simply cannot shoot at a human; and in the meantime while they try to load the guns, they could already be harmed by the criminals. However, if the victims did not have any weapons, instead of fighting back, they could get away and call for help. In other words, when facing criminals, victims are likely harmed if they try to defend themselves. Another study has shown that "a firearm in the home is 43 times more likely to be used for suicide or a murder than self-defense" (Rosen 50). This is understandable since criminals are not present everywhere or any time; hence, guns stored for self-defense purpose would be wrongly used for other violent purposes, which is contrary with the idea of the second amendment. From here, we can see that the main purpose of owning firearms is no longer valid. The purpose to which guns are used as described in the Constitution is outweighed by the purpose to which they are used for violent acts. Therefore, this apparent misuse of firearms provides reason for the gun control laws to be regulated.

Another problem of guns is they increase the rate of gun-related crimes in the United States. Due to the right given by the Constitution, possession of firearms is getting more popular. Consequently, this increases the amount of firearms among the civilians. Therefore, chances of criminals using guns to commit crimes are high. It is believed that if the right to keep and bear arms had been limited, the number of deaths by guns would have decreased. According to Gary Rosen, more than 80 Americans, including about 12 children, continue to die every day due to gun-related incidents (50). Furthermore, in 2007, "32,436 Americans were killed with firearms. In comparison, 33,651 Americans were killed in the Korean War, and 58,148 Americans were killed in the Vietnam War" (Rosen 50). By looking at the statistics, we can easily get the idea why gun regulation is needed. All of these numbers tell that even the people who do not use guns are also killed by guns, including children. This happens because the gun control laws are not strictly limited which makes criminals can easily gain access to guns and commit crimes. In other word, gun control today does not reduce the crime rates. In focus, Gary Rosen states, "The more accessibility to guns you have, the higher the rates of gun-related death and injury" (50). This seems to be true because the number of gun-related deaths are proportional to number of guns are present, which the gun control laws today are aiming to. Based on evidences above, we can infer that the fewer number of guns that are possessed, the lower chances of using them.

People's emotions also cause misuse of firearms. Sometimes people can accidentally commit crimes with guns when they are angry or in a rage with someone. Due to the exposure to violence from TV or video games, some people have aggressive behaviors. Therefore when they are angry, they will probably use guns to solve their problems. In addition, alcohol beverages and drugs also play a great role in the misuse of firearms. Under the influence of alcohol, people are unconscious of what they do. Operating guns in the drunken condition is not so different from drunk driving. A great misuse of firearms is people using them to commit suicide. Due to hopelessness and depression, some people try to end their lives with guns. According to Julian S. Hatcher, Frank J. Jury, and Jac Weller in *Firearms Investigation, Identification, and Evidence*, if guns are not available, people would not easily commit suicide. They write, "The chance of suicide if no firearm is present is relatively remote" (Hatcher 284). Committing suicide with guns is quick and easy. Therefore, people who take pills or hang themselves to commit suicide may have chances to think more before they decide to end their lives. The danger of gun possession is foreseeable if the person who uses gun is not serious-minded.

Keeping guns at home can also cause many unpredictable accidents, especially for children. Gun supporters claim that they keep guns in their homes to defend against thieves and criminals. However, those people have not realized about the risk that guns can easily get into the hands of children, which is greatly dangerous. Misuse of firearms by children who are unaware of the potential danger can lead to serious gun-related accidents. For example, in 2000, a six-year-old boy took a loaded hand gun, which his dad stored at home, to his elementary school in Michigan and shot a six-year-old girl who is his classmate (Rosenblatt). In this case, the man who left the loaded gun at home was castigated for the death. Here, the young boy might not have understood the concept of death. However, he was able to shoot his classmate whom he did not like because he could easily gain access to the gun. Children seem to be curious and interested in guns. The proof is that we can easily notice that young boys prefer to play with gun toys as well as shooting video games. These things make children become more violent and have aggressive behaviors. Therefore, it is possible that children will play with real guns if guns are available in their homes. Moreover, not only are the guns dangerous to children, but the ammunitions are as well. Throwing bullets into fireplaces or hitting them with hard objects will cause explosion which will seriously hurt children. Young children are unpredictable and they are unconscious of the dangerous effects on themselves or their friends. So the possession of firearms is a threat of children's safety.

However, some people believe that it is not easy to buy and own firearms. They say that guns are not sold freely without conditions. In addition, people with negative background checks cannot buy guns. It takes many steps before people can buy guns. There are requirements for people to buy guns such as background checks and licenses. Also, all transactions about buying and selling guns are kept track by the police. In addition, gun-supporters argue that even if guns are banned, murderers and criminals still find a way through the illegal black markets to arm themselves. Jacob G. Hornberger states, "Murderers do not obey restrictions on gun possession, contrary to the long-repeated suggestion of the gun-control crowd — that if we simply enact such restrictions into law, murderers will comply with them." That is, no matter how gun control laws are strict, criminals can still buy guns through the illegal black markets. In other words, people who use guns to commit crimes will also break laws to buy guns. Furthermore, if guns are outlawed in public stores, only criminals and murderers can buy guns from the black markets. The argument of gun-supporters also means that the innocent people who possess guns do not use guns to commit crimes. Gun-related crimes happen because people who use guns are murderers and criminals. In focus, the idea here is criminals indeed will still try to harm people no matter how guns are banned.

On the contrary, what many people do not realize is that the stricter the laws, the fewer the existence of firearms. Today, the conditions required to buy guns just restrict the people who purchase the guns, not those who shoot. We all know that when guns are purchased from the stores, anyone can use guns without any background checks or licenses. That is why keeping guns at home are dangerous to children. Moreover, the illegal black markets are not the places that criminals can simple go there and grab their guns. The risk of being caught of producing, selling, and buying firearms is very high. According to an internet article, "Getting arrested, fined, having property confiscated, or going to jail are all risks of engaging in illegal gun production. This increased risk will cause the supply of guns to fall and the price to rise." ("The Case Against Gun Control"). With all these risks, it is not easy for criminals and murderers to buy guns through these black markets. In addition, with the increase in gun prices, the number of guns purchased by criminals would decrease. Hence, criminals and murderers have less chance of possessing firearms. Moreover, if more gun control laws are enforced on gun ownerships, common criminals like thieves or robbers would have less chance to buy guns. Consequently, the rate of gun-related deaths will decrease. Therefore, it is lucid to say that more gun control laws are needed in order to prevent criminals from having firearms.

Despite the fact that many gun-supporters claim that guns are needed for self-defense, there are many other ways to protect ourselves without having guns. As discussed above, people rarely use guns to fight with criminals. Not everybody can be ready to shoot someone else in defense for themselves or others. In his book about gun control, Gary Kleck states, "Despite this stated willingness of gun owners to shoot under certain circumstances, most defensive uses of guns do not in fact involve shooting anyone." That is, even though people keep guns in their houses, they do not have chance to use guns or they simply cannot shoot at people. Therefore, it is not necessary to possess guns when there are still other ways for self-protection. Also according to Gary Kleck, some other ways to protect ourselves without guns are "locking doors, having neighbors watch one's house, or avoidance behaviors such as not going out at night . . . , maintaining a dog, paying a security guard, buying a burglar alarm system, or relocating one's residence to an area with less crime." With today's technologies, people can have their house wired with alarm systems, which will automatically alert the police or the owners if someone breaks into their houses. Neighborhood watch is also an effective way of security. People in this kind of community will watch for the suspicious activities around the neighborhood at different times to ensure the safety in the community. In focus, people do not need to use firearms in defense for themselves or others.

In general, arguments about the usage of guns and gun control laws in society will continue for a long period of time. However, based on problems stated above, gun control laws should be regulated in order to decrease the rate of gun-related deaths in the United States. The reason for which guns are unnecessary is people are misusing the main purpose of guns possession. Furthermore, for self-defense, people store guns at their homes, which is greatly dangerous to children and unconscious people. The situation would worsen when people use guns as a tool to commit suicide instead of protecting their safety. Besides using guns, there are other solutions for people who need security in their homes. Installing alarm systems in their houses and participating in neighborhood watch programs are the most common ways to secure our houses. Some people argue that guns are just the tools and they do not kill people, but people kill people. However, guns are very dangerous and are used in many criminal activities. In other words, the negative effects of guns outweigh the benefits. Therefore, we can understand that gun possession creates an insecure environment. If gun control laws are well regulated, gun-related deaths would decrease, children would live in a better environment without guns, and the country has less violence.

Works Cited

"2008 Report: Crime in the United States, Expanded Homicide Data." *The Federal Bureau of Investigation*. U.S. Department of Justice, Sept. 2009. Web. 11 Nov. 2010.

Hatcher, Julian S., Frank J. Jury, and Jac Weller. *Firearms Investigation Identification and Evidence*. Harrisburg: Ray Riling Arms Books Company Inc., 2006. Print.

Hoey, Francis. "Gun Control." *Torn By the Issues: An Unbiased Review of the Watershed Issues in American Life*. Ed. Stephen B. Maguire and Bonnie Wren. Santa Barbara: Fithian Press, 1994. 53–84. Print.

Hornberger, Jacob G. "Once Again, Gun Control Doesn't Work." *FFF*. The Future of Freedom Foundation, 18 Apr. 2007. Web. 11 Nov. 2010.

Kleck, Gary. *Targeting guns: firearms and their control.* New York: Walter de Gruyter Inc., 1997. Print.

Rosenblatt, Roger. "The Killing Of Kayla." *Time*. Time Inc., 05 Mar. 2000. Web. 11 Nov. 2010.

Rosen, Gary. "Yes and No to Gun Control." *Commentary*. Commentary Magazine, Sept. 2000. Web. 11 Nov. 2010.

"The Case Against Gun Control." *Libertarian Anarchy*. Libertariananarchy.com, 27 Jan. 2009. Web. 11 Nov. 2010.

Name: _____

Questions

1. What is the author's main argument? What kind of claim is being made? Is this claim effective for this kind of essay? Explain.

   _____

   _____

   _____

   _____

2. Analyze one of the support paragraphs. What kind of support is being used? Is the support effective? Are there any support paragraphs that are not effective?

   _____

   _____

   _____

   _____

3. Discuss the introduction paragraph. Does the introduction hook the reader? Is the thesis clear and arguable? Explain.

   _____

   _____

   _____

   _____

4. Discuss some of the essay's strengths. What does it do well? Be specific.

5. Does the essay have any weaknesses? Explain. How can these weaknesses be improved?

6. Do you agree or disagree with the author? Why? Be specific by referencing the essay. This answer may be written in the form of your own essay.

Chapter 9

Education

At one point, our education system was the best in the world. However, that has changed. Depending on the level of schooling you look at, we rank poorly in basic subjects like math and language skills, but our college system is still highly rated. The concept of education as an argument varies from essay to essay in this chapter. For example, Dolores VanGordon discusses the budget and how it affects schools, teachers, and students. Jeffrey Hunt continues the discussion by arguing how budget cuts directly affect the quality of education. Michael Gonzalez follows with an argument about how to improve our education system in order to remain competitive with the rest of the world. Changing focus, Juana Juarez argues that preschool is an important step in the education of our youth, and she focuses her argument on proving how preschool teaches skills to young learners. Finally, Alex Rollo focuses on the college classroom and argues about the steps needed to create a successful ESL program. Please note that this essay, although still an argument, was written for a different audience and uses APA for all citation.

Dolores VanGordon
English 68
3/3/12

Educational Budget

The educational budget is affecting many Americans. All students nationwide are experiencing the $1.8 billion dollar budget cut (Ceasar). This cut may not show affects on the students' education now, but it will in the future. According to Stephen Ceasar and Teresa Watanabe, ". . . many school districts [have] cut spending for adult education, libraries, textbooks, arts and music, gifted students, tutoring for low-performing high school students and other programs." By eliminating or reducing the availability of these programs, many students are going to struggle with their studies and may even be discouraged to continue their education as adults, since the education for adults is also being jeopardize. The budget cut is taking away funds from much needed educational services because the nation needs to conserve money, which affects students of all ages.

Many students' rely on busses to transport them to school because they live far away and it is unsafe to walk to school, but unfortunately, the budget cannot afford to provide transportation for them. The funding that would have been used to bus children to school is instead being used to salvage the few programs that are left. According to "National Statistics on School Transportation", ". . . one-third of school districts consolidated bus routes to conserve costs, and another third were considering eliminating bus routes or bus stops close to school." In other words, several school districts feel that it is a rational choice to cut transportation for students because students are capable of riding a bike or walking to school, but what the district does not realize is that "Each year, approximately 800 school-age children are killed in motor vehicle crashes during normal school travel hours" ("National Statistics on School Transportation"). This statistic shows that transportation for students is greatly needed and should therefore be included within the school's educational budget.

The education budget cut will affect the future of the United States. Schools are working within a strict budget during the school year and are being forced to decide which programs should stay and which programs should be eliminated. When programs are eliminated, so are the educated individuals who work them. Only then does the public realize that half of Americans that are unemployed are in fact individuals with college degrees. In the long run, the nation will be unable to compete with other countries in education and in marketing. This is important because it stresses that the nation needs to focus on increasing the education budget. According to President Barack Obama, "No issue will have a bigger impact on the future performance of our economy than education'" (Cohen). Obama agrees that schools across the nation should have more funding and that colleges should be more affordable for students. He also feels that education should not be affected during this economic crisis because students need to be as educated as they can. Obama also believes that students are the future of tomorrow and the future leaders of the United States.

Works Cited

Ceasar, Stephen and Teresa Watanabe. "Education takes a beating nationwide." *Los Angeles Times.* Los Angeles Times, 2012. Web. 3 Mar. 2012.

Cohen, Tom. "Obama chides governors for education cuts." *CNN.* Cable News Network, 2012. Web. 4 Mar. 2012.

"National Statistics on School Transportation." *Safe Routes to School: National Partnership.* Safe Routes to School National Partnership, 2012. Web. 4 Mar. 2012.

Name: _____

Questions

1. What is the author's main argument? What is the overall claim being made? Explain.

   _____

   _____

   _____

   _____

   _____

2. Analyze one of the paragraphs. What kind of support is being used? Is the support effective?

   _____

   _____

   _____

   _____

   _____

3. Discuss the flow of one of the paragraphs. Is the topic sentence effective? Does the rest of the paragraph match the topic sentence? Explain.

   _____

   _____

   _____

   _____

   _____

4. Discuss some of the strengths of this assignment. What does it do well? Be specific.

_____

_____

_____

_____

_____

5. Does the assignment have any weaknesses? Explain. How can these weaknesses be improved?

_____

_____

_____

_____

_____

6. Do you agree or disagree with the author? Why? Be specific by referencing the essay. This answer may be written in the form of your own essay.

_____

_____

_____

_____

_____

Jeffrey Hunt
English 68
5/11/2011

The Interdependence of Education and the Economy

Frequently, school budget cuts are made in an effort to reduce the amount of money a governmental body is spending. When a government faces financial crisis, it can be combated by reducing spending and raising revenue. One such example of a measure to fight a large budget deficit was the decision of the California state government to make cuts to public schools totaling nearly 12 billion dollars in February of 2009. Additionally, in the June of the same year, another 5.3 billion dollar cut was proposed. These further proposed budget cuts were made in an effort to alleviate the 24.3 billion dollar deficit the state faced ("State Schools Chief Jack O'Connell Highlights Impact of Budget Cuts to Education"). The total spending on K-12 education from 2005 to 2006 was 36.4 billion ("California Spending Plan 2007-08"). This means that the sum of both the standing and proposed cuts to the school system, 17.3 billion dollars, is about 47.5 percent of the total amount spent on schools during the year three years previous. Many more schools across the world also find themselves at the mercy of economy and government policy, and may not receive enough money to adequately educate students.

The quality of education provided by schools suffers greatly when underfunded. Funding provides schools with the money to buy new equipment and books, run extra-curricular programs, and pay teachers and other employees. Outdated books and computers, inadequate seating, and a shortage of teachers and counselors are not desirable characteristics for a school, and are likely to hinder the progress of students who attend such a school. A 2009 educational budget cut by the state of California provided us with a hard example of the kind of effect underfunding can have on schools; over 26 thousand employees in the California public education system, including 16 thousand teachers, were laid off from their jobs as a result of cuts in the state's education budget. ("State Schools Chief Jack O'Connell Warns State Budget Cuts are Leading to Future Teacher Shortage, Hurt State's Ability to Produce Educated Workforce"). Such a sharp decline in the number of available teachers means that individual class sizes must be raised and non-core curriculum, such as art, music, and foreign languages will shrink. As less time can be devoted to each student and some classes simply cease to be taught, students will, respectively, experience more difficulty in class and have a narrower overall education. Students that are undereducated are more likely to experience difficulties later in life.

Students who are poorly educated as children will become poorly educated adults, who have inherited the responsibilities of their predecessors. The foundation of any society is its people, and as adults grow old and children grow up, the health of a society is governed by the way its newer generations, which must step into power, are taught. The latency of the power shift, however, can make long-term consequences of actions today, like cutting school funding, difficult to assess. The productivity of society as a whole will suffer if its population becomes less educated and less skillful. This means that as schools suffer, societal productivity suffers; as societal productivity suffers, so will economy, and as economy suffers, so will schools. The conclusion of this frightening line of thought is that overall education will continue to decline and the economic hole threatens to grow deeper and deeper. By limiting how much funding is cut from schools, however, properly educated workforces will be allowed to emerge and the cycle will allow for growth rather than decay.

Works Cited

"California Spending Plan 2007–2008." *Legislative Analyst's Office*. Legislative Analyst's Office. Oct. 2007. Web. 11 May 2011.

"State Schools Chief Jack O'Connell Highlights Impact of Budget Cuts to Education." *California Department of Education*. California Department of Education, 3 June 2009. Web. 11 May 2011.

"State Schools Chief Jack O' Connell Warns State Budget Cuts are Leading to Future Teacher Shortage, Hurt State's Ability to Produce Educated Workforce." *California Department of Education*. California Department of Education, 6 Apr. 2010. Web. 11 May 2011.

Name: _____

Questions

1. What is the author's main argument? What is the overall claim being made? Explain.

   _____

   _____

   _____

   _____

2. Analyze one of the paragraphs. What kind of support is being used? Is the support effective?

   _____

   _____

   _____

   _____

3. Discuss the flow of one of the paragraphs. Is the topic sentence effective? Does the rest of the paragraph match the topic sentence? Explain.

   _____

   _____

   _____

   _____

4. Discuss some of the strengths of this assignment. What does it do well? Be specific.

5. Does the assignment have any weaknesses? Explain. How can these weaknesses be improved?

6. Do you agree or disagree with the author? Why? Be specific by referencing the essay. This answer may be written in the form of your own essay.

Michael Gonzalez
English 1A
10-9-11

Schools in America

The education system of the United States, despite being one of the most powerful countries in the world, is mediocre compared to its potential and previous stature. The system is composed of outdated methods that earned it the top rank for education forty years ago. While countries have progressed in increasing there student potential, the United States has focused on ensuring that all their students have a chance at that success. The end result is the slow down of the more talented kid and waste of resources on the students who do not wish to learn. The public education system of the United States is a terribly organized system that should be reformed from the student level and up to its governing region. The younger generations who are constantly put through the American system are put at a disadvantage when competing with countries that are razing there students educations at alarming rates. Without reform, students will continue to lack the skills to advance among there competition and the results will ripple through past and future generations of the American workforce.

American education has faltered over the past decade in attempt to please national standards. The federal government has attempted to intervene in academic affairs in the least way possible. They introduced policies that require schools to meet a certain standard but the interpretation of that policy is left to each state to debate. Each state, in order to collect funds from the federal government, meets the standard but disregard the education resulting in false scores. Mississippi is a prime case where it is stated that 18% of its fourth-graders were proficient in reading, which is the lowest in the country (Isaacson). While the state of Mississippi appeared to be scoring of high degree, it was actually doing worse than other states. The exaggeration of the state of Mississippi is surely not in individual case. Certainly there are quite a few states that do this to meet national standards and receive funds. These false scores are disastrous to our nation's education. States are having their schools look for government aid and ignoring the main function of a school. The relationship between national and state government is a failing relationship but the strain is not just on government but on students and teachers as well.

The roles between student and teachers should not be left in the control of the student to decide. Schools are run by its administration and teachers. Students, however, are influencing the decisions of there mentors. These student influences are making teachers lower their requirements for test, studies, and other work habits. These teachers focus mainly on ensuring that students pass but at the cost of not being prepared with the proper knowledge. Stanton Peele, a PhD graduate and psychologist, writes, "With growing frequency, students at all levels, despite their objectively poor scores, are filing complaints against their instructors for the grades they received—even, often, when these are

'B's or even 'A's. . . ." Peele identifies that a majority of American students do receive low scores and complain and that teachers in return attempt to satisfy the students' request. Instead of the student improving his knowledge so as to pass, the teacher gives a merciful passing grade. If education is the focus than a student should get the proper scores deserved. Students should learn from these mistakes to improve there skills. There is an undeniable issue when teachers can not complete there work effectively and damage the learning experience of their students.

Another new policy that should be enforced is the review of teachers to prove their efficiency at there job. Teachers in public schools have lost there effectiveness of past decades after losing their focus on adaptive teaching and switching to following terribly designed curriculums. The fear of judging teachers effectiveness is a sensitive subject due to the many teacher unions. However, there fear of opposition from teachers and there unions may be over hyped. Walter Isaacson asks the question of reform to teachers and unions and finds that they would not oppose. He receives a response from the American Federation of Teachers saying that a set of clear guidelines would provide high quality teachers and curriculum to the high schools (Isaacson). Even teacher unions recognize a problem and believe that their teachers should be reviewed. The removal and retraining of the teachers would benefit them in allowing for more pleasant defined working environments. The call for reform is heard not just from the people, the students, but the teachers and their organizations as well. Each agrees that we are falling behind, and soon the international community will surpass us if we fail to adapt.

The American education system should be able to compete on the international level. The country has one of the most available public education system and cache of resources in the world. However, the nations position has faltered by disorganized management and undefined standards. Diane Ravitch, a historian of education and New York University, says, "In assessments of math and science, U.S. performance is mediocre. On the math portion of the TIMSS, our eighth-grade students rank 16 of about 46 nations. On the PISA test, American scores in science and math literacy were below the average for the 30 nations of the Organization for Economic Cooperation and Development. We spend a lot of time on education—only Sweden spends more—so these outcomes are disappointing." There is an obvious issue in the method academics are being taught if we put the most time into teaching and yet we are still overcome by other countries. If we were to put in as much time as we do and include the key traits of the leading nation's successes than The United States could be capable of being the top ranked international country. This, however, will not occur as long as America continues down its current path of its outdated system. If America wants to become the highest ranked country for education than it must look towards progress.

The necessity for education reform is undeniably crucial to the future of United States. With governments focused on money and not on education, students, teachers, and communities continue to suffer. The system between the education are so damaged that teachers have lost sight of there true responsibilities to their students. Even worse is how districts and teaching organizations have failed to provide their teachers with guidelines in benefiting themselves and the future generations of America. The terrible state of the education system has left us in a dim view to those the international community that is quick to judge the once might superpower. If the country does not learn to adapt to the every changing skill of teaching than surely the affects will be felt across the globe as the American education system continues to crumble.

Works Cited

Isaacson, Walter. "How to Raise the Standards in America's Schools." *Time Magazine.* Time Inc, 2011. Web. 9 Oct. 2011.

Peele, Stanton. "A Problem America Won't Solve in our Lifetime: Education." *Psychology Today.* Sussex Directories, Inc, 2011. Web. 11 Oct. 2011.

Ravitch, Diane. "Question & Answers: The Truth About America's Schools." *The American.* American Enterprise Institute, 2010. Web. 11 Oct. 2011.

Name: _____

Questions

1. What is the author's main argument? What kind of claim is being made? Is this claim effective for this kind of essay? Explain.

   _____

   _____

   _____

   _____

   _____

2. Analyze one of the support paragraphs. What kind of support is being used? Is the support effective? Are there any support paragraphs that are not effective?

   _____

   _____

   _____

   _____

   _____

3. Discuss the introduction paragraph. Does the introduction hook the reader? Is the thesis clear and arguable? Explain.

   _____

   _____

   _____

   _____

4. Discuss some of the essay's strengths. What does it do well? Be specific.

5. Does the essay have any weaknesses? Explain. How can these weaknesses be improved?

6. Do you agree or disagree with the author? Why? Be specific by referencing the essay. This answer may be written in the form of your own essay.

Juana Juarez
English 101
May-18-11

The Importance of Going to Preschool

How important is to go to preschool? Preschool can be a half or full day program for young children from 3-5 years old. It could be a state or federal founded or private program. Preschool is a program where young children can develop self and social development, language and literacy, cognitive, mathematical development, English language development, and health skills that will help them succeed in their future education. Some preschool programs have learning foundations and alignment components that are associated with each individual and unique child that has both social and academic outcomes. The California Preschool Foundations are preschool standards that some preschool programs use as a framework. Some preschool programs use these foundations as a framework to be in alignment with Desired Results Developmental Profile (DRDP) assessment. Preschool is a valuable opportunity to enrich the lives of children and prepare them for their proceeding education. High quality preschool programs feature a wide variety of fun activities such as singing, dancing, arts and crafts, storytelling, free play, and both indoor and outdoor games and projects designed to teach children different skills. Children also learn academic concepts related to numeric comprehension and literacy. Most preschool programs require teachers have a degree in early childhood education and follow licensing regulations. Preschool is a developmentally appropriate program that younger children should assist. Developmentally appropriate means understanding and being knowledgeable about how children grow, develop and learn; moreover, taking into account individual differences and needs, as well as social and cultural constructs. This is important because children that attend preschool programs are more prepared academically and emotionally before starting kindergarten, they are accustomed to a certain level of structure and a classroom routine. Furthermore, children have the opportunity to socialize with other children their age.

Attending preschool can make a significant difference in children's language development. Children typically can make themselves understood when they communicate with familiar adults and children. At the preschool age (3 to 5), they may make pronunciation errors or sometimes use words in unusual ways that are understood by people who know them, but not by people who are not familiar with them. Preschool teachers can support young children's language development by repeating and extending what children say in conversations. In preschool, children are exposed to storybook reading, both of wordless pictures books and regular books. Book sharing and reading enhances children language because the book is used as a tool to develop language. In preschool, children also learn and expand their vocabulary. They also acquire vocabulary through teacher-guided activities. Children learn much of their vocabulary and basic language concepts indirectly through their interaction with others. Dixie Abbot, Janet Lundin, and Faye Ong write, "In preschool, children are developing the ability to use language for a range of purposes, such as describing, requesting, commenting, greeting, reasoning, problem solving, seeking new information, and predicting" (49). In preschool children develop language through music, phonological awareness chants, syllables, rhymes and as they play. Children become increasingly skilled at remembering and practicing the language modeled around them. They can go from saying just a few words to suddenly producing full sentences in just a short matter of time. Attending to preschool children can learn language and more.

Another benefit of preschool is that children learn how to socialize with their peers. People are not conscious that socialization is a continuing process whereby an individual acquires a personal identity and learns the norms, values, behavior and social skills appropriate to their social position. In the preschool classroom teachers create opportunities for children to practice how to take turns, cooperate, share, problem solve, build a positive self-concept, follow directions, use good manners, and respect others. They are exposed to active, hands-on, age-appropriate, meaningful experiences. Most of the preschool teachers provide guidance for conflict resolution encouraging children think independently best way to solve the conflict taking others feelings into consideration. Preschool teachers also teach social skills by modeling and then reinforcing social skills concepts through role-playing. Roberta M. Berns writes, "However, reciprocal interactions in the peer group don't usually begin until about age of 3, when the child starts to understand the views of others and, therefore, is able to cooperate, share and takes turns. Cognitively, the child is beginning to move away from egocentrism . . ." (51). Preschool children start preschool at age of three, so is the perfect age when they are cognitively ready to understand the rules of socialization. Socialization occurs through experiencing and interacting and there is no other right place where children can learn socialization skills than preschool.

In addition to language and socialization by going to preschool children will learn the alphabetic and word/print recognition. Recognizing letters is a basic step in the process of learning to read and write. In order for children to have a good start recognizing the alphabet letters, parents need to take them to preschool. In the preschool classroom environment, children are exposed to letters everywhere and every day. For example, children wear nametags at school. This will help them begin to recognize and become familiar with the letters in their name. As children become aware of the names of letters, they also begin to identify printed words. In addition, knowing the names of the letters facilitates children's ability to decode text and to apply the alphabetic principle to word recognition. Abbot writes, "Some children who have well-developed knowledge of the alphabet and letter-sound correspondences, coupled with relatively good phonological awareness, may read at partial alphabetic levels during the preschool years" (83). Children learn through play with hands on; therefore, in the preschool classroom children sing the alphabet song along with the sounds, have letter magnets, white boards and dry eraser markers, chalks, and journals. They can use these materials during free time also during planed activities by teachers. Preschool teachers provide many kinds of games and appropriate activities that support children with the ability to remember the sounds associated with the letters.

Furthermore, in preschool, children begin to understand numbers and quantities in their everyday environment; in other words, children in preschool learn math abilities that will help them prepare for later in number recognition, measurement, geometry, and algebra. In the preschool setting, teachers support children's learning at different levels. Teachers introduce mathematics through songs, calendar, flannel stories, finger puppets, counting games, and number related books. Preschool provides children with access to developmentally appropriate, challenging and engaging materials. Children have the opportunities to count different objects in the classroom; to explore and compare objects' sizes, shape, weight, and other attributes; to measure; to sort and classify; and to discover and create patterns. Abbot states, ". . . young preschool children are becoming aware that objects can be compared by weight, height, or length and use such words as "heavier," "taller," or "longer " to make comparisons" (146). The experience that takes place during the preschool years is very helpful for young children to learn mathematics. It is the time when children learn to recite the numbers in order, recognize numerals, and begin to incorporate the idea of one-to-one-correspondence and true counting. Furthermore, math naturally takes place throughout the preschool classroom and throughout the day. Children explore objects and learn about shapes and numbers as they go about their daily routine for example, doing the calendar, counting present and absent boys and girls, at snack time and while they play in different areas in the classroom.

Another benefit preschool can bring is the early identification of children with special needs. In preschool teachers assess the children through observations and planned developmentally appropriate activities. Everyday activities done in the preschool classroom have different developmental purposes for children. Many of them are to expose children to manipulate, explore, experience, or to observe a specific outcome. However, when teacher observes that a specific child is demonstrating behavior signs such us, no eye contact, attention span, biting, hitting or isolated child, she knows right away that something is going on. She immediately starts collecting evidence and fills out a referral form. After the parents are informed of their child's concern, schools need to obtain parental consent to do all the necessary testing and assessments to determine if the child needs help or an Individualized Educational Plan (IEP). Ruth E. Cook writes, "Exploration, manipulation, expression, sharing, and active involvement provide easy opportunities for educators to structure and reinforce meaningful interactions between children with disabilities and those without" (233). Parents may not be equipped at home with the require material to do all the assessments, so they could not meet their children needs. However, in preschool the professionals are properly equipped to help children with disabilities plus these children are exposed to play and learn from different peers. Some disabilities in children are lucid. For instance, Down syndrome, behavior and speech, these needs are more visible and many people can notice easily. On the other hand, some others are dubious like Autism and Attention Deficit Disorder (ADD) these problems are not easily to identified and preschool is the right place where children can be identified by a professional, and obtain the necessary help. Preschool teachers have special challenges; one of them is to help children with special needs to realize their full human potential. By recognizing the human similarities in each child and by positively valuing differences giving them the opportunity to develop their unique strengths.

Another positive effect of going to preschool is that children learn how to follow a classroom routine. Most of the preschools have a daily routine schedule, so when children do the transition to kindergarten, they will know that the classroom has rules to follow. As a result, they will know what to expect when kindergarten teacher mentions that is time to do large group, small group, free choice, outside time, line up and lunchtime. They will know how the management system works and all the different consequences when they misbehave in the classroom. In addition, typically children that go to preschool do not experience separation anxiety because they have become used to getting dropped off at preschool. A kindergarten teacher in a personal interview was sharing the differences between children that went to preschool than the children that did not go. Cervantes said, "I have been working for twenty years in a kindergarten classroom, and I can easily identify children that went to preschool. They do not cry the first day of school; they listen and follow the rules in the classroom." Children who know the classroom routine and rules can be more effective learners because they have school experience and know how to follow teacher's instructions. Kindergarten teachers that take experienced preschoolers will focus on their task and that way fulfills teacher expectations.

It is argue by some parents that early childhood programs are unnecessary and inappropriate because children do not learn academics skills, like reading neither numbers. They argue that children that go to preschool only play throughout the school year. Some parents request that in order for their children to go to preschool, this programs should have direct instruction. According to an Internet article, Brown states, "'Teaching numbers, teaching letters, teaching facts through direct instruction will get you better test scores.'" Some parents are not agreeing with the playing philosophy in preschool and they do not believe that children learn through play. They want their children learn how to write letters and numbers with proficiency then read if will be possible. Brown writes, "That proficiency is measured on tests, but the far-reaching effects of play do not show up in answers to multiple-choice questions." Some parents are agreeing to send their children to preschool, but setting the rules that they do not want to send them to waste their time playing. Preschool educator Kathy Blythe say, "Some of mi students parents want their children learn how to write their names correctly using the lower and upper case letters. They also want their children to recognize numbers and to count as high as they can." Parent's expectations are that preschool teachers prepare their children academically and they keep asking about alphabet letters and numbers whenever the have the opportunity to talk with their children's teacher. In other words, some parents are not agree with the preschool programs because their children are not learning academics and they complaint because children only go to preschool to play for most of the time.

What parents do not know is that children at the preschool age (3-5) are not ready to learn academics and their learning is through play with hands on. As children enter the preschool years, they begin to explore the world trough indirect experiences such as drawing, building with blocks, dance, music, pictures, and crafts. All these experiences help children expand their knowledge and understanding of the world while developing eye-hand coordination and other motor skills. According to an Internet article, "Through play, children develop gross motor skills (physical mobility and muscle control) and fine motor skills such as eye-hand coordination a critical precursor to reading and writing skills. Equally important, play helps make learning fun! . . ." ("The Link Between Play and Learning"). Parents who are complaining about playing in preschool need to know more about children developmental stages, so that they will understand why children learn more through active exploration and social interaction. Play is the foundation for children's imagination and sparks creativity, making the learning journey pleasurable and joyous. Toys are fun, but toys are also tools that help children learn about themselves and the world around them. Play is critical to the healthy growth and development of children. As children play, they learn to solve problems, play stimulates the imagination, it also contributes to develop confidence, self-esteem, a sense of the children's own strengths and weaknesses, and a positive attitude toward learning. Parents need to understand the importance of play in preschool. Being more involved in early education will help them to know more about human development, thus, they will comprehend why play is an important role in preschool.

In conclusion, children are tremendously benefit-attending preschool. Attending to preschool children not only learn and expand vocabulary, but many other things as well. Socialization is another benefit that children practice while they are in a preschool classroom. In addition, children start naming and recognizing the alphabet letters and their sounds as well as recognizing and reciting the numbers in order. Moreover, in preschool children with special needs are identified and properly helped. Finally, the transition to kindergarten is easier for preschool children because they have experience in the classroom routine. It is true that some parents argue for more direct instruction and less play in preschool. However, they are not aware of the developmentally appropriate practices that preschool children have to develop before they start with the direct instruction. Clearly, the most viable effect that children have going to preschool is to let them play. Parents also need to speculate the benefit that playing contributes to all the learning methods. Understanding the positive effects of going to preschool and how it helps, parents should take advantage and sent their children. Furthermore, children will be better preparing for their coming school years.

Works Cited

Abbot, Dixie, Janet Lundin, and Faye Ong, eds. *California Preschool Learning Foundations.* Vol. 1. California: California Department of Education, 2008. Print.

Berns, Roberta. *Child, Family, School, Community: Socialization and Support.* California: Wadsworth/Cengage Learning, 2010. Print.

Blythe, Kathy. Personal Interview. 13 May 2011.

Brown, Emma. "The Playtime's the Thing." *The Washington Post.* Format Dinamics, 21 Nov. 2009. Web. 25 Nov. 2009.

Cervantes, Kate. Personal Interview. 08 May 2011.

Cook, Ruth E., Diane M. Klein, and Annette Tessier. *Adapting Early Childhood Curricula for Children with Special Needs.* 7th ed. New Jersey: Pearson Merril Prentice Hall, 2008. Print.

"The Link Between Play and Learning." *Northern Illinois University.* Board of Trustees of Northern Illinois University, 2011. Web. 13 May 2011.

Name: _____

Questions

1. What is the author's main argument? What kind of claim is being made? Is this claim effective for this kind of essay? Explain.

   _____

   _____

   _____

   _____

2. Analyze one of the support paragraphs. What kind of support is being used? Is the support effective? Are there any support paragraphs that are not effective?

   _____

   _____

   _____

   _____

3. Discuss the introduction paragraph. Does the introduction hook the reader? Is the thesis clear and arguable? Explain.

   _____

   _____

   _____

   _____

4. Discuss some of the essay's strengths. What does it do well? Be specific.

5. Does the essay have any weaknesses? Explain. How can these weaknesses be improved?

6. Do you agree or disagree with the author? Why? Be specific by referencing the essay. This answer may be written in the form of your own essay.

Alex Rollo
Master's Synthesis
August, 2010

NOTE: This essay is adapted from the synthesis project, *A Ten-Week Low-Intermediate Level Adult English as a Second Language Course Curriculum* which was presented to the faculty of the Kalmanovitz School of Education at Saint Mary's College of California in August of 2010. To develop a thorough scope and sequence on which a curriculum for a ten-week, low-intermediate level adult English as a Second Language course could be based, a lesson plan pilot was developed, implemented, and evaluated. This project began with the discovery of why such a scope and sequence needed to be developed. Past research covering pedagogy and content design was then analyzed and conclusions were drawn to form the scope and sequence. In accordance with the scope and sequence, a lesson plan pilot was developed and underwent a one-week implementation and evaluation. Three instructors and 22 students from one adult intensive English language program in San Francisco, California participated. The final project also included a one-week lesson plan framework that a ten-week course curriculum could emulate.

The Need for a Standardized Curriculum within English Language Programs

There are more than one billion people learning English; 750 million are learning English as a foreign language (in a country where English is not the spoken language) while 375 million are learning it as a second (in a country where English is the spoken language). More than one-sixth of the world's population can be considered students of the English language. From this large sample, there is, unsurprisingly, a constant stream of customers willing to pay high prices to gain English skills they cannot learn on their own. There are more than twenty for-profit English programs in San Francisco teaching English to financially sound adult foreigners of all ages and backgrounds. Students enroll in high-priced, for-profit English programs with the expectation that they will speak English fluently upon completion of the program. As with commercialized products in general, there exists an underlying belief that the more expensive a school is, the better a student's English skills will become.

Within Adult Intensive English Language Programs (AIELPs), teachers are solely responsible for equalizing the English as a Second Language (ESL) teacher-ESL student relationship, and they are to do so without adequate compensation. The teachers' inability to do so as a result of not being given the tools necessary results in students being cheated of a deserved and decent education. Paulo Freire (2004) stated that "Education must begin with the solution of the teacher-student contradiction, by reconciling the poles of the contradiction so that both are simultaneously teachers and students." To solve the problem of this teacher-student contradiction, the only possibility for teachers within for-profit programs to reconcile "the poles of the contradiction" is to provide their students with the education the students deserved - whether it is because they paid for it or simply because they desire it. This provision means that teachers have to devise their own curriculum, a process that is nigh on to impossible for a number of reasons. The amelioration of this problem is of the utmost concern.

There exists an industry wide issue, the lack of agreed upon standards when it comes to Adult Intensive English Language Programs' (AIELP) definition of English as a Second Language (ESL) education. AIELPs have no concrete, universally applicable, and appropriate coursework. The teachers within the field are mostly empty-handed and forced to reinvent the wheel every time they enter the classroom. Many teachers are left to fend for themselves without having been provided a well-developed curriculum or even basic guidelines. In many cases, ESL teachers employed within AIELPs are not provided with the necessary materials to effectively run a classroom.

The problem does not end there. After close scrutiny of job posting websites (Craigslist, ESL Café, SFGate, CATesol) and for-profit program employee handbooks (School A, School B, School C, School D), two more issues surfaced related to the for-profit AIELP business plan. First, there appears to be a significant disconnect between management and the design or implementation of the materials necessary to effectively teach the customers. Within job postings and handbooks, no statements are made regarding the curriculum being implemented. Managers appear not to have spent sufficient time developing specific student learning outcomes or standards. Educators are left without any knowledge of what the program is striving to achieve in terms of the education of its students.

The second issue, just as prevalent, is the fact that for-profit programs are not requiring their teachers to possess any teaching experience or certification. These traits are only "preferred." Skills listed as "required" consist of only a Bachelor's Degree as well as some form of people skills and time commitment. Neither experience in an ESL classroom nor a post-secondary degree in a related field is required. Programs are not taking the steps necessary to guarantee that teachers possess the skills necessary to effectively instruct an ESL class, especially a class without a predetermined curriculum. According to job postings seen on employment opportunity websites (SFGate, Craigslist; CATesol; ESL Cafe) and company websites (School A; School B; School C; School D), teachers are paid $18-$20 per teaching hour, a wage that does not include any pay for time spent outside the classroom, even if that time is spent on the preparation necessary for class. This income amount does not entice teachers to spend their limited free time deciphering their program's teaching material. The result is teachers who are unprepared for class and students who are not receiving what they have paid for and deserve.

The curricula of four international AIELPs clearly reflect these inadequacies. Two programs provide the teacher with one textbook and the instruction to implement one chapter per week (School A; School B). Without professional interpretation, the chapter encompasses just one day's worth of material, but teachers are expected to fill a week's worth of classes. At another school, a ten-week curriculum is written on one page declaring only the subject matter and grammar point for each week leaving the teacher to first articulate what is being asked and then to find appropriate activities. The material is simply a scope and sequence of standards and forms presented in a format that an untrained ESL teacher is unlikely to be able to effectively interpret (School C). Another program provides only guidelines as to what instruction each level should provide but nothing in regards to how to do so or under what timeline it should be done (School D).

For those teachers who do possess the skills to interpret the materials, the interpretation of the standards and outcomes requires significant uncompensated time outside of class because there is no place where a teacher can find an all-inclusive curriculum reflecting the materials that have been provided. Nowhere can they find a curriculum aligned with the recommended scope and sequence of language development based on necessary standards and forms. Teachers need to research each piece separately on their own time.

To solve the problem of the imbalanced business plans within AIELPs, programs must offer teachers an adequate and well-explained standards-based curriculum. This curriculum needs to include a clear presentation of the learning outcomes as well as provide activities that could be used to support those outcomes. From the perspective of AIELP management, the curriculum needs to be financially feasible, one that does not result in any loss of profit. The curriculum can satisfy this requirement by not requiring any further creative effort on the part of the AIELP in that no payment for work hours is needed.

From the perspective of the student customers, the curriculum must be effective in that they actually learn from it. A students' education is the ultimate goal of any classroom instruction; therefore, the conclusion that student needs must be satisfied (Reid, 1987) should act as the catalyst and justification for all curricular development. Contrary to the current school of thought, there is no single curriculum that is adequate for all learners, no matter their similarity in age. Reid's (1987) conclusion, though obvious, is extraordinarily complex since student needs vary widely, according to such factors as mother tongue, education level, culture, gender, and age. This fact has to be taken into account so that the course plan can accommodate the students' different learning needs. The major point of Reid's findings is that pedagogy must be culturally sensitive. Curriculum developers must consider that an adult ESL learner, like any learner, is a complex individual, and a classroom of complex individuals requires an equally complex curriculum.

The solution is a corporeal standards-based comprehensive course curriculum inclusive of well-defined objectives that can go into the hands of educators. The curriculum should fill the void described above, equipping both experienced and novice teachers with a highly structured guide to effectively achieving the educational objectives of the course. If the developmental curriculum is to satisfy the needs of all those involved, the creation of the curriculum must stem from an understanding of the end goal, begin with the end in mind (Covey, 2004), referred to as backwards mapping in the field of education (Wiggins & McTighe, 1998). The scope and sequence should cover three equally important areas: authenticity (Roberts & Cooke, 2009), form and function (Dutro, 2008), and theme (Eskey, 1984, 1992). It must result in cognitive skills (Cummins, 1994,

1996) developed through communicative activities (the theory of Communicative Language Teaching: Savignon, 1991; Nunan, 1989, 1991, 1995) centered on authentic themes (Eskey, 1984, 1992). Likewise, it must attempt to satisfy the needs of both the teacher (Gandara et al., 2005) and student (Reid, 1987).

A course curriculum which reflects each of these crucial aspects for teachers within an AIELP will enable those teachers to better and more consistently educate their students. Thus, the AIELP would need to spend less resources training and supervising its staff. The AIELP could rely on the fact that a tool implementable by all teachers and effective for all students was being administered in its classrooms. Those programs that adopt such a standardized curriculum may benefit by having better prepared students who are satisfied with their education experience and represent the program well. These "satisfied customers" may then recommend the program to others. Therefore, the AIELP could spend more time focusing on other aspects of company development and profit making.

Likewise, the creation of such a course curriculum will almost certainly have an implication for the students. The students will benefit by having effectively sequenced, carefully articulated, and consistently applied curricula across their program of study. From program commencement, students will have a clear picture of learning outcomes and learning expectations throughout their enrollment in the program, a foundational need of the adult learner. Finally, the most important implication of these suggested curricula is for the teacher. The teachers benefit by not feeling isolated and unguided in their curricular development. Upon entry into the classroom, teachers will have a clear picture of what to teach and how to teach it. In short, the teachers' ability to begin with the end in mind would lead to a happier Adult Intensive English Language Program, for teachers, students, and administrators, alike.

References

California Teaching English to Speakers of Other Languages job postings, 2010. Retrieved May 23, 2010 from www.CATesol.com

Craig's List job postings, 2010. Retrieved May 23, 2010 from www.CraigsList.org

Cummins, J. (1996). The two faces of language proficiency. In Negotiating identities: Education for empowerment in a diverse society (pp. 51–70). Ontario, CA: California Association for Bilingual Education.

Cummins, J. (1994). Knowledge, power and identity in teaching English as a second language. In F.

Dutro, S. (2008). A focused approach to systematic English language development: A handbook for elementary teachers. Santa Cruz, CA: ToucanEd.

Eskey, D. (1984). Content: The missing third dimension in syllabus design. In Read, J. (Ed.) Case studies in syllabus and source design (pp. 65–79). Singapore: SEAMEO Regional Language Centre.

Eskey, D. (1992). Syllabus design in content-based instruction. In Snow, M. & Brinton, D. (Eds.). The content-based classroom (pp.132–141). New York: Longman. English as a Second Language Café job postings, 2010. Retrieved May 23, 2010 from www.ESLCafe.com

Freire, P. (1970). Cultural action for freedom. The Harvard Educational Review; Monograph Series, 1, Cambridge: Harvard Educational Review.

Freire, P. (2004). Pedagogy of the oppressed, 30th anniversary edition. (M.B. Ramos, Trans.). New York, NY: The Continuum International Publishing Group, Inc. (Original work published 1970).

Gandara, P., Maxwell-Jolly, J. & Driscoll, A. (2005). Listening to teachers of English language learners: A survey of California teachers' challenges, experiences, and professional development needs. Santa Cruz, CA: The Center for the Future of Teaching and Learning.

Nunan, D. (1989). Designing Tasks for the Communicative Classroom. Cambridge: Cambridge University Press. 1989.

Nunan, D. (1991). Communicative tasks and the language curriculum. TESOL Quarterly, 25(2), (pp. 279–295).

Nunan, D. (1995). Language teaching methodology. London: Prentice hall.

Reid, J. (1987). The learning style preferences of ESL students. TESOL Quarterly, 21(1), (pp. 87–111).

Roberts, C., & Cooke, M. (2009). Authenticity in the adult ESOL classroom and beyond. TESOL Quarterly, 43(4), (pp. 620–649).

Savignon, S. J. (1991). Communicative Language Teaching for the twenty-first century. In Celce-Murcia, M. (Ed.) Teaching English as a second or foreign language, third edition (pp. 13–28). Boston: Heinle & Heinle.

San Francisco Gate job postings, 2010. Retrieved May 23, 2010 from www.SFGate.com

Wiggins, G., & McTighe, J. (2005). Understanding by design, 2nd edition. Alexandria, VA: Association for Supervision and Curriculum Development.

Wiggins, G., & McTighe, J. (1998). Understanding by design, 1st edition. Alexandria, VA: Association for Supervision and Curriculum Development.

Name: _____

Questions

1. What is the author's main argument? What kind of claim is being made? Is this claim effective for this kind of essay? Explain.

_____

_____

_____

_____

_____

2. Analyze one of the support paragraphs. What kind of support is being used? Is the support effective? Are there any support paragraphs that are not effective?

_____

_____

_____

_____

3. Discuss the introduction paragraph. Does the introduction hook the reader? Is the thesis clear and arguable? Explain.

_____

_____

_____

_____

_____

4. Discuss some of the essay's strengths. What does it do well? Be specific.

5. Does the essay have any weaknesses? Explain. How can these weaknesses be improved?

6. Do you agree or disagree with the author? Why? Be specific by referencing the essay. This answer may be written in the form of your own essay.

Chapter 10

Internet

The Internet is such a modern concept; arguments involving laws and the management of the Internet are new and changing every day. The Internet, and all that it brings, is part of our lives, integrated through our computers, cell phones, and entertainment devices. But what does all of this mean? Can the Internet be both a positive and negative force in our lives today? Samantha Zayas believes that the Internet is a useful tool and proves that it has a positive impact on our lives. On the other hand, Alejandra Martinez argues that the Internet can be dangerous, and she focuses on the new topic of cyber bullying between today's youth.

Samantha Zayas
English 68
February 3, 2011

The Internet: A Useful Tool

The Internet is a revolutionary invention for most students, since it is a convenient source when doing research. The Internet provides thousands of sources on nearly every topic conceivable. Students can research a specific topic for their schoolwork without the tedious task of going to the library, searching for books, and reading the books. Jenny Bronstein is a professor at Bar Ilan University (Israel) with a doctorate on social technologies from the Department of Information. Bronstein writes, "Studies found the accessibility of networked sources so decisive that students use the Internet as their primary source of information as a matter of convenience." The Internet has become students' number one resource for research. Without leaving the comfort of their home, students are able to access hundreds of credible, informative websites. By simply typing a few keywords into an online search engine, students receive thousands of potential reference sources, such as articles, encyclopedias, blogs, and videos. Also, these sources are short in length and condense with information, which saves students time. In addition, the Internet is usually accessible twenty-four hours a day, seven days a week. Therefore, students can obtain information about their topic at midnight if they must. As a result, the Internet is a beneficial resource to students who are in need of researching.

Furthermore, the Internet is also a marvelous invention for students who are researching information to support their argument, as the Internet provides the most recent and valuable articles on virtually every topic. When researching, most students want to know the most current information about their topic. With this information, students are able to write a more centralized essay to prove their argument better. By creating a strong argument, students are more likely to receive a higher grade from their professors. According to Mark Ko, who is the senior editor of the website *Upublish.info* and has many years of experience in the fields of business, marketing, and security, "the Internet offers . . . [a]ccess to new and valuable sources of information that came into being because of the Internet." Printed books provide reasonable information; however, due the time required to write, edit, and publish the book, the information in books is usually outdated by three or more months. The Internet, on the other hand, is updated daily; thus, the Internet provided students with the most recent statistics, scientific advancements and discoveries, and news reports. In addition, Internet sources such as *Time*, *CNN*, *Los Angeles Times*, *Yahoo*, *Webmd*, and *Health Affairs* contain many articles that are detailed on the topic a certain student is researching. This is an essential to students as they are able to utilize the information to create a persuasive argument that is supported by specific evidence and that directly correspond with their topic and today's society. As a result, the Internet is an important resource for students researching information because the Internet contains many recent articles that can support a student's argument.

Works Cited

Bronstein, Jenny. "Selecting and Using Information Sources: Source Preferences and Information Pathways of Israeli Library and Information Science Students." *Information Research* 15:4 (2010). 25 Oct. 2010. Web. 2 Feb. 2011.

Ko, Mark. "Benefits and Drawbacks of the Internet as a Research Source." *Article Garden*. Article Garden, 2010. Web. 1 Feb. 2011.

Name: _____

Questions

1. What is the author's main argument? What is the overall claim being made? Explain.

   _____

   _____

   _____

   _____

   _____

2. Analyze one of the paragraphs. What kind of support is being used? Is the support effective?

   _____

   _____

   _____

   _____

   _____

3. Discuss the flow of one of the paragraphs. Is the topic sentence effective? Does the rest of the paragraph match the topic sentence? Explain.

   _____

   _____

   _____

   _____

4. Discuss some of the strengths of this assignment. What does it do well? Be specific.

5. Does the assignment have any weaknesses? Explain. How can these weaknesses be improved?

6. Do you agree or disagree with the author? Why? Be specific by referencing the essay. This answer may be written in the form of your own essay.

Alejandra B. Martinez
English 68
February 10, 2011

Why the Internet is Dangerous

Have you ever wondered what teenagers are doing on the internet so long? Why they are so caught up with being online most of the time? Parents know that most teenagers today spend hours on the Internet. What they do not know is what their children are doing on the Internet and how they are damaging their health. There are children whose activities online are more dangerous than their activities at school or at home. Some children are harassed online while others are the ones doing the harassing. Cyber bullying has become common among adolescents and is more damaging than the traditional type of bullying. Cyber bullying has made the Internet more dangerous for children and teenagers.

Some children's activities on the Internet involve being bullied, otherwise known as cyber bullying. Based on the definition of cyberbullying by *About.com*, "Cyberbullying is any harassment that occurs via the Internet. Vicious forum posts, name calling in chat rooms, posting fake profiles on web sites, and mean or cruel email messages are all ways of cyberbullying." Bullying has passed from the school yard to every child's home. Bullying is no longer an action that victims can escape. Today bullies can use the internet to harass their victims, which creates a bigger problem for society. According to Sameer Hinduja and Justin W. Patchin, authors of *Bullying Beyond the School Yard: Preventing and Responding to Cyberbullying*, some children become bullies online because:

> First electronic bullies can remain "virtually" anonymous. Temporary e-mail accounts and pseudonyms in chat rooms, instant messaging programs, and other Internet venues can make it very difficult for adolescents to determine the identity of their aggressors. An individual can hide behind some measure of anonymity when using a personal computer or cell phone to bully another individual, which aids in freeing the individual from traditionally constraining pressures of society, conscience, morality, and ethics to behave in a normative manner. (20)

Because cyber bullying gives bullies a certain level of anonymity, more children are going to attack online than in person. Online bullying also lets the bully get away with the harassment because the victim might not know who the attacker is. The more bullies exists the more victims there are.

Because cyber bullying has become common among teenagers and children more and more are at risk of being bullied. Unfortunately, not every child talks to somebody when they are being harassed online. Most teens and children only talk to their friends and seek suggestions from their peers. The *Los Angeles Times* article, "Cyberbullying Affects 40% of Kids," written by Nina Sparano states, "According to the Cyberbullying Research Center, 40% of kids in the U.S. say they've been bullied on the Internet . . . For every cyberbullying incident you read about, like last week's suicide of a Rutgers University student, Tyler Clementi there are at least a half-dozen that never make headlines." Nearly half of the teenagers in America are been bullied, and only a few bullies are punished for their actions. The most common bullies that are punished are those who lead their victims to suicide and end up making it on the news headlines.

Unlike conventional bullying, cyber bullying is an action that can scar a victim for life. With conventional bullying, the victim can move with their family to another town and the bullying can stop. As the person grows up, they might just forget what happened when they were younger. The article, "Cyberbullying," written by *Kids Health from Nemours* states, "Severe cyberbullying can leave victims at greater risk for anxiety, depression, and other stress-related disorders. In very rare cases, some kids have turned to suicide." Cyber bullying can cause an emotional strain on the child being bullied as well as push them to the point of suicide. According to the article "Cyber bullying Statistics," on the website, *Bullying Statistics*, "Cyber bullying can be very damaging to adolescents and teens. It can lead to anxiety, depression, and even suicide. Also, once things are circulated on the Internet, they may never disappear, resurfacing at later times to renew the pain of cyber bullying." Sometimes when a child is being bullied, online they get a bigger audience and that might make the child feel more stressed. Since the bully can reach its victim at any time of the day, the child might feel like there is no way out and end up committing suicide.

School should be allowed to punish cyber bullies to stop the bullying from going any further. More than likely the bullying started at school and was taking into the online realm, giving school another reason to get involved in the punishment of an online bully. Unfortunately, some schools and parents do not agree that the school should take action when children are being bullied online because the bullying is happening outside of school premises. In the article, "Online Bullies Pull Schools Into the Fray," by Jan Hoffman, she interviews two principals who were faced with the conflict of punishing cyber bullies:

> "I said, 'This occurred out of school, on a weekend,'" recalled the principal, Tony Orsini. "We can't discipline him."
> "I have parents who thank me for getting involved," said Mike Rafferty, the middle school principal in Old Saybrook, Conn., "and parents who say, 'It didn't happen on school property, stay out of my life.'"

While there are schools that are glad to get involved and try to put an end to bullying, there are schools that are not sure if they should get involved because the bullying is not happening in school. The same idea goes with parents. There are parents who want the school to get involved and help put an end to bullying, but there are parents who think the school should not get involved because the bullying is not happening at school.

Regardless of whether the bullying is happening in school or at home, schools can get involved and teach children how to stay safe when they are online. There are many books aimed to teach a curriculum of how to surf the Internet with out putting one self in danger. Books like *Cyber Bullying: A Prevention Curriculum for Grades 3–5*, written by

Susan P. Limber, PD.D. in collaboration with Sue Limber and *Cyber Bullying: A Prevention Curriculum for Grades 6–12*, also written by Susan P. Limber help:

> . . . raises awareness of what cyber bullying is and why it is so harmful, equips students with the skills to treat people respectfully when using cyber technologies, gives students information about how to get help if they or other are being cyber bulled, and helps parents now what to do to keep their children safe from cyber bullying . . . it provides background information and step-by-step instructions on how to implement the curriculum.

Even when schools might not get involved in punishing the bullies, there is always something schools can do to help the victims of cyber bullying. Holding an assembly once or twice a semester to teach some of the thing in the books mentioned above might help stop bullying.

The use of the Internet has a negative impact on children's lives. It puts many children and teens in danger. Some children are victims of cyber bullying, and other children are the cyber bullies. Cyber bullying has a negative effect on children's lives and can even lead them to suicide. Unfortunately, many schools do not like to get involved because the bullying is not happening in school. Even when the bullying is not happening in school, schools can teach their students what cyber bullying is and how they can get help if they are victims.

Works Cited

"Cyber bullying Statistics." *Bullying Statistics.* Bullying Statistics- Stop Bullying, Harassment, and Violence, 2009. Web. 12 Feb. 2011.

"Cyberbullying." *About.com.* About.com, 2011. Web. 9 Feb. 2011.

"Cyberbullying." *Kids Health form Nemours.* The Nemours Foundation, 2011. Web. 10 Feb. 2011.

Hinduja, Sameer and Justin W. Patchin. *Bullying Beyond the School Yard: Preventing and Responding to Cyberbullying.* California: Corwin Press ASAGE Company, 2009. Print.

Hoffman, Jan. "Online Bullies Pull Schools Into the Fray." *New York Times.* The New York Times Company, 2010. Web. 13 Feb. 2011.

Limber, Susan P. and Sue Limber. *Cyber Bullying: A Prevention Curriculum for Grades 3–5.* Minnesota: Hazelden, 2009. Print.

Limber, Susan P. *Cyber Bullying: A Prevention Curriculum for Grades 6–12.* Minnesota: Hazelden, 2008. Print.

Sparano, Nina. "Cyberbullying Affects 40% of Kids." *Los Angeles Times.* Los Angeles Times, 2011. Web. 11 Feb. 2011.

Name: _____

Questions

1. What is the author's main argument? What kind of claim is being made? Is this claim effective for this kind of essay? Explain.

   _____

   _____

   _____

   _____

2. Analyze one of the support paragraphs. What kind of support is being used? Is the support effective? Are there any support paragraphs that are not effective?

   _____

   _____

   _____

   _____

3. Discuss the introduction paragraph. Does the introduction hook the reader? Is the thesis clear and arguable? Explain.

   _____

   _____

   _____

   _____

4. Discuss some of the essay's strengths. What does it do well? Be specific.

_____

_____

_____

_____

5. Does the essay have any weaknesses? Explain. How can these weaknesses be improved?

_____

_____

_____

_____

6. Do you agree or disagree with the author? Why? Be specific by referencing the essay. This answer may be written in the form of your own essay.

_____

_____

_____

_____

Chapter 11

Television, Video Games, and Other Media

Like the Internet, media (and all of its subtopics) are constants in our lives—we are bombarded by some kind of media almost everyday. It is everywhere and what it means to our society can be argued from nearly every perspective. In this chapter, students will argue about television and video games, both of which include violence, language, content, and how all of these affect those who watch it. Gabriela Ruiz begins by arguing that all forms of media should be considered a form of entertainment and not educational. Alejandra Martinez then focuses on video games and what parents can do to prevent their children from watching the violence depicted on the screen. Gabriela Lara continues the argument by showing how laws and restrictions help parents buy the right game(s) for their children. The topic of video games continues in Brian Zajicek's essay, which explains the addiction to video games, and why this problem needs to have solutions in order to help future generations. Finally, Carlos Fuentes argues that there is no evidence that violent video games affect the children that play them, which counters all the arguments of the previous authors. Do violent games affect children? Is violence on the TV screen bad for us? Read these paragraphs and essays and then decide for yourself.

Gabriela Ruiz
English 101
20 June 2011

Media: Is it Really Beneficial?

When it comes to the controversial topic of media, Antonia Peacocke believes that one needs to be knowledgeable in order to understand the deeper meaning that television shows aim to transmit. In her essay, "Family Guy and Freud", television shows are more than entertainment; they are a chance to exercise the brain without thinking of it as work. The shows requires attention in order to understand why the characters act and say they things they do because they have more than one purpose. Likewise, when a characters makes jokes, one needs to analyze it in order to comprehend the intended purpose. Peacocke states, ". . . those who pay more attention and think about the creator's intentions can see that *Family Guy* intelligently satirizes some aspects of American culture" (261). In making this reference, Peacocke argues that when one lacks the ability to analyze the purposes of the scripts, they do not recognize that the jokes have a deeper meaning that relate to today's philosophies. Moreover, the programs stimulate the brain without putting the pressure of and instructional atmosphere. Television requires for one to use their brain in order to appreciate the shows that are broadcasted.

The media has many ways of projecting their different benefits, whether it is by shows in televisions or articles in magazines. Television and magazines open one's mind in order to gain knowledge in a different way other than in school. Articles also follow the techniques used in educational literature, which then exposes students to different writing styles. For example, Gerald Graff, author of the book *They Say/I Say with Readings*, agrees with Peacocke, and he furthers his opinion by using magazines as an example. He believes that when reading something of interest such as magazines, not books that are required, one gains more knowledge because it requires intellectual thinking and one can relate to them. It makes it easier to understand and learn the writing structure because the subjects of the columns are appealing to the public. In his essay, "Hidden Intellectualism", he maintains that "Sports after all was full of challenging arguments, debates, problems for analysis, and intricate statistics that you could care about . . . [he] believe[s] that street smarts beat our book smart in our culture . . . because they satisfy an intellectual thirst more thoroughly than school culture, which seems pale and unreal" (301). The essence of Graff's argument is that one does not necessarily need to read dull and fictional information in order to become skilled at communicating a point of view in writing. Furthermore, "street smarts" is not something that could be taught in a classroom because every individual has a different way of viewing culture and of learning how to adapt to it. Graff makes a clear point that intellectual knowledge is not only acquired in school, but also in one's interests such as magazines.

By focusing on some of the benefits of media, the dangerous consequences are overlooked. The media portrays a false assumption about life and does not bring knowledgeable information. There is a reason why schools were built, they were designed to educate and make rational civilians. Books, not magazines, were created to instruct the public in order to progress and become coherent members of the society. In an article called, "Television and Children", by Kyla Boyse, she states, ". . . audiences can come to view the world as a mean and scary place when they take violence and other disturbing themes on TV to be accurate in real life." This proves that ignorant spectators get frightened because they believe the world is a "bad" place due to the content of the programming in television since they air realistic events, but they do not stop to think that those are paid actors. The false portrayal of society through television leads the viewers to have untruthful assumptions about life and their surroundings which alters their way of thinking. The media's only purpose is to entertain and should not pretend to be educational.

Works Cited

Boyse, Kyla. "Television and Children." *University of Michigan Health System.* Regents of the University of Michigan, 2011. Web. 17 June 2011.

Graff, Gerald. "Hidden Intellectualism." *They Say/I Say: With Readings.* Gerald Graff, Cathy Birkenstein, and Russel Durst. New York: W. W. Norton, 2009. 297–303. Print.

Peacocke, Antonia. "Family Guy and Freud." *They Say/I Say: With Readings.* Gerald Graff, Cathy Birkenstein, and Russel Durst. New York: W. W. Norton, 2009. 257–266. Print.

Name: _____

Questions

1. What is the author's main argument? What is the overall claim being made? Explain.

   _____

   _____

   _____

   _____

   _____

2. Analyze one of the paragraphs. What kind of support is being used? Is the support effective?

   _____

   _____

   _____

   _____

   _____

3. Discuss the flow of one of the paragraphs. Is the topic sentence effective? Does the rest of the paragraph match the topic sentence? Explain.

   _____

   _____

   _____

   _____

   _____

4. Discuss some of the strengths of this assignment. What does it do well? Be specific.

5. Does the assignment have any weaknesses? Explain. How can these weaknesses be improved?

6. Do you agree or disagree with the author? Why? Be specific by referencing the essay. This answer may be written in the form of your own essay.

Alejandra B. Martinez
English 68
January 27, 2011

Video Games: Can They Be Stopped?

Videogames are a bad influence for children when used without monitoring. Most parents allow their children to play with out the parent knowing how the video game is rated or the amount of violence in the game. This can lead to children playing violent video games and learning inappropriate behaviors. For example, in her article, "Do Video Games Really Spark Bad Behavior," Daniel J. DeNoon states that Psychologist Elizabeth Carll says, "Generally, the research shows that violence in video games increases children's aggressive behavior and decreases their helpful behavior . . . [kids] become more aggressive and less empathic." Violent video games desensitize children by teaching the child how to kill people. When children are only learning how to kill or say bad words through their video games, they are more likely to act on those behaviors. In other worlds, the child is less likely to do something nice, because the video game is not teaching the child how to be nice. It does not mean that the child is going to go around killing others, but the child is more likely to get into fights at school or be more aggressive.

Parents can do many things to keep their children from playing inappropriate video games. Children should not be allowed to spend hours on end playing video games. One way to solve video game "problems" is for parents to buy their children age appropriate video games. In DeNoons article, Psychologist Carll also states, "It is important for parents and educators to review what the kids are viewing and to teach them. When someone gets killed, the parent could say, 'You know, this is just a game, and the dead person comes back the next time you turn on the game. . . .'" Since parents are the ones that buy the video games', they should be looking at how the game is rated and learning what all the symbols mean. Parents should also be watching what the child is playing from time to time and giving them time limits to play. When parents watch what their children play it gives them a chance to explain things about the video game. One of the things the parent could explain is why it is not appropriate to use the same language the characters use in the video game. They also need to explain the meaning of death, and why they should not kill someone in real life; as oppose to the game, where the child is being rewarded for killing. Even though video games can have a negative affect on children, parents can step in and do things differently avoid the negative impact.

Works Cited

DeNoon, Daniel J. "Do Video Games Really Spark Bad Behavior." *FOXNEWS.com*. Fox News Network, LLC, 2011. Web. 26 Jan. 2011.

Name: _____

Questions

1. What is the author's main argument? What is the overall claim being made? Explain.

   _____

   _____

   _____

   _____

   _____

2. Analyze one of the paragraphs. What kind of support is being used? Is the support effective?

   _____

   _____

   _____

   _____

   _____

3. Discuss the flow of one of the paragraphs. Is the topic sentence effective? Does the rest of the paragraph match the topic sentence? Explain.

   _____

   _____

   _____

   _____

   _____

4. Discuss some of the strengths of this assignment. What does it do well? Be specific.

_____

_____

_____

_____

_____

5. Does the assignment have any weaknesses? Explain. How can these weaknesses be improved?

_____

_____

_____

_____

_____

6. Do you agree or disagree with the author? Why? Be specific by referencing the essay. This answer may be written in the form of your own essay.

_____

_____

_____

_____

_____

Gabriela Lara
English 1A
29 Sept. 2011

Is Violence in the Media Really "Bad" for Us?

Violent video games should be put on the market only after many restrictions have been applied to ensure that the young audience is steered clear of them at local stores. Video games and consoles are must have for many in the new technology world which can be of use to a certain point, but when violent games get in the hands of small children, it really can be disastrous. Violent video games have become very popular because modern day graphics depict the very real gore that would similarly happen in real life if one was to act out certain acts of violence such as killing someone. Violent video games depict very cruel images that can be very harmful and very much influential to a child at a young age. Kids are easily entertained and even more easily manipulated which is where these inappropriate games take fault. Kids develop ideals of what they believe is right or entertaining and are inclined to act out what they see which is where one can see violent games take role in the every day life. When a young child intentionally or accidentally plays a game where, "options include eating an opponent's head, pulling out their stomach after spitting acid down their throat and slicing them in half with a buzz saw" as seen in *Mortal Combat*, kids will over time be desensitized to real emotions and actions in the real world (Gross). This is extremely important to understand because such violent games affect the psychological thinking of a child's developing mind in a horrible way. Kids grow up believing that violence and gore is okay to replicate in real life situations. Players get rewarded for bad behavior and therefore, children will grow up feeling accomplishment at the act of cruelty because they grew up believing it to be very normal. Young children develop the mind set that acting out anger and frustration with such harsh actions will allow them to express themselves when truly, actions like those reflected in the games would realistically land them in jail for a very long time if not for life. Makers of such games should realize that violent games serve no purpose and only harm the psyche of the audience who it is intended for and even of the younger audience who it should be kept away from. There should most definitely be stricter regulations on games rated for mature audiences only so that parental figures are at all times aware of the things that their children are exposed to, especially when it comes to under aged kids.

Parents can only do so much when it comes to supervising video game activities that their children do therefore, there should be stronger regulations in place to assure that the level of violence is nowhere near influential if a minor was to play with no parental guidance. Kids, especially younger ones, see something that they can not have and are immediately more inclined to do or have. It is human to be attracted to the forbidden but this is a very dangerous situation because not only is it bad to lie to parental figures, but it is bad that one gets influenced to enjoy cruelty. Most parents do their best to be involved in their child's activities but the reality is that not one parent can regulate every activity that a child does within the day. Kids are left alone to do as they please and these are the circumstances where kids get in trouble, and in this case, play games that are not rated for their specific age. Games are all rated accordingly but this is not enough regulation to bind into a game. Most parents buy their child the game that they beg for without reviewing it or taking the time to see why it is rated "mature" and so on. The problem is that kids can be exposed to these games elsewhere, and there should be certain regulations to how much violence even the greatest rated games should have because one never knows who will end up playing it. For those "ignorant" parents who do not take interest on what their child makes them purchase, there should be regulations within the game itself: "Hopefully, though, parents will notice the 'M for Mature' rating on the cover, just to the left of the dude wielding a bloodied chainsaw" (Gross). Because some parents whether concerned or not involved can not be around all day, there needs to be a limit on how much cruelty can be portrayed in the game. This is a crucial point to examine because the fact that children are exposed to violent games is more likely to happen when there are no parental figures around. Levels of criminal activity, killing, torture, and aggressive sexual content should be highly minimized on games that are rated for an older audience. Young children take liking to such games because they get a sense of rebellion when alone or nowhere near parental figures. If high rated violent video games were more strictly regulated, many problems within the society could be diminished. By regulating even the worst games in the market, peace of mind would be distributed to all parental figures trying to raise young kids in a violent dominated world, and a more mentally stable state would in turn exist for growing children everywhere.

Works Cited

Gross, Doug. "The 10 biggest violent video-game controversies." *CNN*. Cable News Network, 2011. Web. 26 Sept. 2011.

Name: _____

Questions

1. What is the author's main argument? What is the overall claim being made? Explain.

_____

_____

_____

_____

_____

2. Analyze one of the paragraphs. What kind of support is being used? Is the support effective?

_____

_____

_____

_____

_____

3. Discuss the flow of one of the paragraphs. Is the topic sentence effective? Does the rest of the paragraph match the topic sentence? Explain.

_____

_____

_____

_____

_____

4. Discuss some of the strengths of this assignment. What does it do well? Be specific.

5. Does the assignment have any weaknesses? Explain. How can these weaknesses be improved?

6. Do you agree or disagree with the author? Why? Be specific by referencing the essay. This answer may be written in the form of your own essay.

Brian Zajicek
English 68

Virtually Addicted

Whether or not one enjoys playing them, video games have become so integrated into our society that they cannot be ignored. They have a huge fan base that includes anyone, from small children, mothers, and teenagers to movie stars and athletes. Video Gaming has gone from something that was thought of as only for the socially inept, to a worldwide phenomenon. It would be a tough task to go somewhere in modernized countries and find an area where not even one person has played a video game. But just because it has become such a popular way of entertainment, does not mean that it is without its flaws. Video gaming is an extremely addicting past time. It has the potential to take a normal, social person, and suck so many hours out of their day that they become friendless and unhealthy. People need to begin to realize how addicting this hobby has become, and find a solution to the problem as soon as possible. If they do not, video gaming has the potential to take over many people's lives and limit their ability to become successful, physically fit, and may remove many other opportunities that they may want to achieve.

It is clear that video games can become an addiction when abused. But what exactly addiction means, and the types of addiction that come along with video games may be confusing. *Random House Dictionary* defines addiction as, "the state of being enslaved to a habit or practice or to something that is psychologically or physically habit-forming, as narcotics, to such an extent that its cessation causes severe trauma" ("Addiction"). Even though being addicted to video games is much different than being addicted to drugs, many video games can be just as habit forming and can get someone hooked on them in a similar way. People who have an excessive need to play video games can be addicted to them in many forms. Some people can get addicted to the social networking involved in many games. Others get addicted to the fierce competition in games. While still others get addicted to the feeling they have of escape that comes with playing video games. Video games have many addicting aspects, and many video games are made in order to fully maximize their additive potential, so more and more people play these games.

But how exactly does one go about finding out if someone is addicted to video games? The problem here lies in the fact that scientists are not quite sure how to locate the exact point where a person goes from a person who plays video games to a person who is addicted to video games. In a study by ABC news about how many hours some of the most zealous players spend on video games, they found that, "these 'extreme' gamers are playing more than 45 hours per week" (Phillips). This shows how many hours an avid video gamer plays, but it is not clear if these individuals are addicted or not. Although the exact amount of hours of playing needed to tell if someone is addicted is unclear, people addicted to video games show symptoms such as, "Alterations in normal schedule and sleep patterns to free up time to play; avoidance of other activities that were once pleasurable; dropping friends and relationships in favor of game playing" ("Video Game Addiction Diagnosis"). There are also more obvious symptoms like spending excessive amounts of money on video games. These are obviously self-destructive behaviors that can hurt a person's life in a terrible way if not checked. People who study video gaming and their effect on people need to focus more attention on finding out if a person is an addict or not, so that they can receive as much help as they can, as early as they can.

Many video game companies understand that this addictive quality in video games is true, and they strive to make money off of it. Some companies even create games that can be played indefinitely, where there is an ever expanding game universe with more and more to accomplish. These types of games fuel gamers' addictions. For some video games, such as MMORPGs (or Massive Multiplayer Online Role Playing Games), it is the game's focus to keep the player coming back, day after day, and month after month, because the way the companies make their money is off of a subscription fee. One example of this type of game is *World of Warcraft*. According to an article about this video game, "World of Warcraft currently has 9.3 million subscribers. Estimates in psychological fields suggest that anywhere from 10% to as high as 40% of these players could be addicted. This translates to anywhere from 930,000 to 3,720,000 people addicted to WoW [*World of Warcraft*]" (Richford). That is a large amount of people who waste a large portion of their life sitting in front of a television or computer screen doing nothing other than playing this game. But to the companies that make the game; these people are loyal customers who they can count on for guaranteed revenue. Video game companies who prey on people with addictive personalities just to earn money should understand that what they are doing is not right. What they are doing is potentially ruining peoples' lives by basically taking them over. Even if the people who are addicted enjoy themselves while over-playing, it does not justify the potential pain that might come out of it.

Playing video games can have a wide range of negative effects on the people who enjoy them in excess. Many addicts can be stricken with these different consequences, and further hurt themselves more than just taking up a lot of their social life. These consequences can gravely affect the person who is playing in devastating and potentially lethal ways. Some of the physical effects that have a chance to strike chronic video gamers are, "obesity, video-induced seizures. And postural, muscular and skeletal disorders, such as tendonitis, nerve compression, and carpal tunnel syndrome" (Gentile). All of these issues are a resultant of both the actual playing of the video games, and the way that people who play video games hurt their bodies by ignoring health promoting activities. The more and more people play video games, the more and more likely it is that these disorders may occur. And once one of these issues has occurred, it is easy for another one to take effect, or for one of them to develop into a more health threatening condition. Sadly though, this is not the only negative effect that video games can have on a person.

Video games can also have a large effect on a person's mentality. One of the biggest and most controversial effects is considered to be whether or not video games increase violent behavior in people who play them. Since many video games have graphic depictions of violence, it is believed that, due to their immersive and interactive nature, they can easily influence and desensitize people into thinking that such acts are okay to do in society. According to the American Academy of Child & Adolescent Psychiatry, "Studies of children exposed to violence have shown that they can become: "immune" or numb to the horror of violence, imitate the violence they see, and show more aggressive behavior with greater exposure to violence" ("Children and Video Games: Playing with Violence"). Even though this study is about children it actually affects adults too since these children will grow up with these types of attributes in their personalities. Even though the effects are less than those on children, witnessing or committing virtual acts of violence can promote real life violence amongst adults as well, just as movies or television do. Since the 'greater exposure to violence' causes more and more of this unacceptable behavior, the people who are most at risk are the addicts. With violent behavior and more of a chance to imitate violent acts, addicts are just adding more and more adverse attributes to their condition. In this situation though, video game addiction is not just potentially hurting themselves and those close to them, but it is actually putting a strain on society itself by introducing people with more violence into the world.

One example of an addict who hurt society by committing acts of violence he learned from a video game was Devin Moore. *60 Minutes* did a report on the video game *Grand Theft Auto* and the negative effects it had on the young adult who took the game's ideas and brought them into real life. They reported, "The game is at the center of a civil lawsuit involving the murders of three men in the small town of Fayette, Ala. They were gunned down by 18-year-old Devin Moore, who had played *Grand Theft Auto* day and night for months" (Leung). Moore, who was obviously addicted to this video game, had killed three policemen who were interrogating him about stealing a car earlier that day. When he was caught and asked why he did it Moore responded, "Life is like a video game. Everybody's got to die sometime" (Leung). This is a clear case of one video game addict that took his obsession with these games too far. It is quite possible that if Moore had not been addicted to video games and had not been as desensitized to violence as he was, these crimes would not have occurred. Since this kind of addiction can lead to so many negative effects, something must be done in order to stop people from either hurting themselves from playing too much, or hurting other people by committing crimes they have learned from playing violent video games.

One solution to the problem of addiction is putting limits on the time people can play video games. Since the main negative effect of people getting addicted to video games is gratuitous amounts of time being consumed in a non-productive manner, the best way to fix or limit video game addiction is to set a fixed amount of time that people can play video games. For example, on games like MMORPGs, the companies can set a limit on how long a person can log in the game over the period of a week. And for games that are played on home consoles, the manufacturers can set a game time limit, so that if people pass the time limit, it saves the game and kicks them off, and while the game playing functionality is disabled, the console can still be turned on and run DVDs and other media. Before this occurs though, people need to study how long is too long for gaming, and how long is 'just enough'. If the 'just enough' time can be found, it will allow gamers to have the right amount of time to play a game and enjoy it, but not allow them to overdo it and allow it to be abused. This is essential to helping video gamers who are addicted because it can give them enough time to clear their heads and practically force them to find other things to do rather than play video games. It also limits the amount of interactive violence that they receive from video games that may cause them to become violent themselves. There is also one more solution that will likely to fix the problem of video game addiction.

The other solution to video game addiction is video game rehabilitation. Although it is not as wide spread or available as drug rehabilitation, video game rehab can still help addicts grow past their problems and learn to beat the addiction. Some people may not know how serious video game addiction can be. The type people who need to be checked into this kind of facility tend to be the type of video game addicts that make their game world a higher priority than hygiene and personal health. These clinics are, "staffed with certified psychologists and addiction specialists that can offer legitimate help to those unwilling to leave their games to have a social life or even use the bathroom" (Horaczek). Specialized psychologists and addiction specialists are exactly what many video game addicts need. These specialists will help the person realize that their excessive use of video games has become a problem, and that without help, they may put their health, life, family, and friends either in danger, or so close to the brink of failure that it would be impossible to get them back. Video game rehabilitation is not as wide spread as it should be, and if people want to be able to help these addicted gamers get their life together, then the rehabs need to more available to the public and easily accessed.

Some of the people, who do not agree with the fact that video games have a negative influence on players, believe that they actually are a learning tool that can help people in their everyday life. Playing many video games requires a high degree of problem solving and a quick mind. The more and more people play these games the sharper their ability to do complex actions becomes. When ABC news did a study on how video games can benefit people of today they said, "In the modern world of fast decision-making, e-mail and e-trade, games might be helping develop the kinds of skills . . . to succeed" (Berman). These kinds of skills can be used in order to get ahead in many jobs that require brain power. And since many of today's jobs focus on technology, a person who is as familiar with technology as most video gamers are, should easily adapt and work well in that type of environment. Social critic and author, Steven Johnson said, "They're out learning how to think in ways that will be absolutely useful to them when they go out in the world and do the same kind of thinking in an office" (Berman). This kind of thinking can include thinking out of the box, fast reactions to problem causing events, quick analysis, and other beneficial tools that many employers look for when they want to hire new applicants. Therefore, playing video games regularly (and proficiently) means that the player will actually receive more benefits when he/she move into the real world of jobs and money making, rather than hindrances. This shows that the benefit of video gaming may possibly outweigh some of the negatives that were presented above, and make avid player's lives better than not playing games.

Although some video games do cause people to get ahead in life, most of them cause people to fall behind. And what the people who believe that video games are actually good for people fail to realize is, that people who play video games, and especially people who play them excessively, have more of a chance to end up in a place where they are unprepared for what life has to offer. This is because people who are addicted to video games are more likely to do worse in school compared to those who are not. Douglas Gentile, an article writer for a parenting help publication, states, "Simply put, the amount of time spent playing video games has a negative correlation with academic performance." When being interviewed for a job, one of the first and most important things that the interviewer looks at is how much and what kind of education a person received prior to the job interview. With poor academic performance the player will have a harder time getting into any college at all, let alone a good college. Thus, if the addict is in an interview for a prestigious job, he or she will be less likely to be hired if there is someone with a higher education competing with them for the job. With a low education the only type of positions readily available are those for fast food restaurants and entry level retail positions that earn minimum wage. So, in reality, playing too many video games will not make one prepared for future life, but actually lead them on a road to mediocrity.

Video games obviously can have a large negative effect on those who play them too much. People who play them form an addiction which leads them to a place, where they actually will have a negative reaction if they stop playing for a long time. Even though it is clear that video gaming can become such a destructive force in a person's life it is hard for people to determine when video games go from enjoyable past time, to severe addiction. Also, many video game companies do not help the addiction by purposely designing their games to be played for an unlimited amount of time, in order to make a profit. Because video gaming can become a real addiction, there are a wide variety of negative effect that come along with it. Some of the physical and psychological problems are carpal tunnel, obesity, seizures, and even increased violence in the players. And as seen in the case of Devin Moore, these negative effects can cause serious problems for society as well as the individual playing the games. Luckily though, some of these problems can be fixed if people took initiative. A few ways of doing this can be limiting gaming time, and video game rehabilitation. Although the harmful aspects of video games are clear, there is still a group of people who believe that video games can actually help someone in their life. Their argument states that playing video games help with problem solving and thinking outside of the box with technology, which will give them an edge in the office environments. But this is refuted with the fact that video games actually cause people to have a poor schoolwork ethic, causing them to have lower, and preventing them from getting higher class jobs. This all goes to show that even though gaming is a worldwide entertainment medium, it can actually do a lot of harm to people who take it too far.

Works Cited

"Addiction." *Random House Webster's Dictionary*, Revised Edition. 4th ed. 2001. Print.

Berman, John. "Do Video Games Make Kids Smarter?" *abcNews*. ABC News Internet Ventures, 2 June 2005. Web. 25 May 2010.

"Children and Video Games: Playing with Violence." *American Academy of Child & Adolescent Psychiatry*. American Academy of Child Adolescent Psychiatry, Aug. 2006. Web. 26 May 2010.

Gentile, Douglas. "The Effects of Video Games on Children: What Parents Need to Know." *BNET*. CBS Interactive Inc., June 2004. Web. 24 May 2010.

Horaczek, Stan. "Rehab Center For Video Game Addicts Opens In Amsterdam." *Engadget*. AOLNews, 15 July 2006. Web May 24 2010.

Leung, Rebecca. "Can A Video Game Lead to Murder?" *CBS NEWS*. CBS Interactive Inc., 19 June 2005. Web. 25 May 2010.

Phillips, Ashley. "Study: 'Extreme Gamers' Play 45 Hours a Week." *abcNews*. ABC News Internet Ventures, 11 Aug. 2008. Web. 25 May 2010.

Richford, Nannette. "World of Warcraft Addiction: Fact or Fiction." *Associated Content*. Associated Content, Inc., 22 Nov. 2007. Web. 25 May 2010.

"Video Game Addiction Diagnosis." *MyAddiction.com*. MyAddiction.com., 2010. Web. 24 May 2010.

Name: _____

Questions

1. What is the author's main argument? What kind of claim is being made? Is this claim effective for this kind of essay? Explain.

_____

_____

_____

_____

2. Analyze one of the support paragraphs. What kind of support is being used? Is the support effective? Are there any support paragraphs that are not effective?

_____

_____

_____

_____

3. Discuss the introduction paragraph. Does the introduction hook the reader? Is the thesis clear and arguable? Explain.

_____

_____

_____

_____

4. Discuss some of the essay's strengths. What does it do well? Be specific.

5. Does the essay have any weaknesses? Explain. How can these weaknesses be improved?

6. Do you agree or disagree with the author? Why? Be specific by referencing the essay. This answer may be written in the form of your own essay.

Carlos Fuentes
English 67
November 2, 2011

Violence Caused by Video Games

There is no scientific research to validate a link between video games and violent behavior. Violent behavior can be influenced by other factors like the environment, family background, and imposed morals. Numerous studies shown in books and journals, such as "Grand Theft Childhood: The Surprising Truth About Violent Video Games, And What Parents Can Do" by Cheryl K. Olson, Sc.D. and Lawrence A. Kutner, Ph.D. and "Do Video Games Kill?" by Karen Sternheimer, have proven that there is no connection that violence can be a product of playing video games. Cheryl K. Olson stated, "It's clear that the 'big fears' bandied about in the press—that violent video games make children significantly more violent in the real world; that children will engage in the illegal, immoral, sexist and violent acts they see in some of these games—are not supported by the current research . . ." (18). Violent crime has gone down in these past 20 years while video game sales have done nothing but go up. These facts show the fallacy of linking violent behavior and games to be nothing more than people always needing to blame something.

The public should not put the blame on media, like video games, television, music, and movies, whenever there is a violent incident, but instead try to figure out what other factors could have caused the violence. It is easy to find things to blame when things unexplainably go in the wrong direction. Christopher J. Ferguson writes, "When tragedies such as the Columbine High School shooting occur, it is tempting to look for 'scapegoat' answers to a complex problem" (11). Throughout history, when no clear answers could be found at a given in time, people would just find things to blame like religion or the youth. In conclusion, even if there is evidence showing video games do not cause violent behavior, the ignorance of people will continue blaming video.

Works Cited

Ferguson, Christopher. "Evidence for publication bias in video game violence effects literature: A meta-analytic review." *Aggression and Violent Behavior* 12.4 (2007): 470–82. Print.

Kutner, Lawrence and Cheryl K. Olson. *Grand Theft Childhood: The Surprising Truth About Video Games And What Parents Can Do*. New York: Simon & Schuster, 2008. Print.

Name: _____

Questions

1. What is the author's main argument? What is the overall claim being made? Explain.

_____

_____

_____

_____

2. Analyze one of the paragraphs. What kind of support is being used? Is the support effective?

_____

_____

_____

_____

3. Discuss the flow of one of the paragraphs. Is the topic sentence effective? Does the rest of the paragraph match the topic sentence? Explain.

_____

_____

_____

_____

4. Discuss some of the strengths of this assignment. What does it do well? Be specific.

5. Does the assignment have any weaknesses? Explain. How can these weaknesses be improved?

6. Do you agree or disagree with the author? Why? Be specific by referencing the essay. This answer may be written in the form of your own essay.

Chapter 12

Obesity

America is the fattest country in the world. Obesity is a serious problem that brings with it serious health risks. What causes obesity and what effects it has on our lives will be discussed in these essays. The argument is this: Whom do we blame for obesity in America? Is it our fault for choosing what to eat, or does the fast food industry play a part in this "growing" problem? First, Verna Trujillo discusses obesity and children because children are greatly affected by being obese. In addition, children cannot always decide what to eat, so there must be something done to protect them. Next, Samantha Zayas traces the exact causes of obesity today and clearly blames fast food for the medical problems we face. Kevin Russell argues that despite our ability to choose what to eat, the government still has a duty and role to play in regulating the fast food industry. Finally, Wylie McGraw places the blame on us—we are capable of making choices and what we choose to eat affects the obesity rate in this country. Between laws set by the government and our right to choose, we can fight obesity and live healthier lives.

Verna Trujillo
Eng. 1C
February 11, 2010

Childhood Obesity

Billy Robbins weighs 800 lbs, consumes approximately 30,000 calories in a day, and is a high school senior. Billy struggles to get up from the chair he spends most of his days on, has a difficult time walking, and needs assistance when using the restroom, normal day activities that an average weight teenager could easily accomplish. Billy has said that he not being able to do anything for himself leaves him feeling like he is a prisoner in his own body (Fry). Billy is not the only obese child fighting obesity in the United States. In 2009 there were 74.9 million children, ages 0–17, living in the United States and 16 percent of those children are obese ("POP1 Child population: Number of children (in millions) ages 0–17 in the United States by age, 1950–2008 and projected 2009–2021"). That is an astonishing 11,984,000 million children battling obesity in America today. There are many serious health problems the child will encounter as an adult that results from being an obese child. Not only does it affect their physical health but it also affects them emotionally and socially. Childhood obesity will greatly impact our society because these are the children that will one day lead the country. Children who are obese often have low self esteem and remove themselves from social situations. We want our children to be proactive and productive in their lives as adults so they can give back to society in a beneficial way. Therefore, if there is nothing done to help prevent the problem of childhood obesity then obesity in children will greatly increase within the next five years.

However, some experts do not feel that childhood obesity is a problem to be examined more carefully. Many people believe this because they feel that there is little evidence to support the health effects of an obese child. In Paul Campos' book, *The Obesity Myth Why America's Obsession with Weight Is Hazardous to Your Health*, he tells a story about a child named Anamarie who was average weight when born but over the next three years gained over 120 pounds and grew twice as tall as children her age. Anamarie's doctors could not figure out why she had grown so rapidly and gained so much weight within three years. Her parents were told that "Ana's in grave danger . . . And we don't want her to die down the line" but could not give them an explanation as to why (Campos 100). Campos writes:

> The story of Anamarie Regino tells us a great deal about the meaning of fat in America today. It tells us that, for all its pretensions to knowledge, the medical profession still understands very little about the causes and consequences of much of what is labeled 'obesity' . . . no one knows if her size endangers her health (how could anyone know this, given the complete failure to diagnose the nature of the underlying condition?). (104)

Campos' point is that after three years, fifty-seven appointments, and three overnight hospitalization stays, the doctors, who were so concerned for Anamarie's health, could not diagnose her with a problem. The doctor's assume that their knowledge of obesity can greatly affect the child but have no such proof of the consequences. As a result of Anamarie's story, many people have concluded that doctors do not always know the reasons for childhood obesity and its affects it can have on the child.

I strongly disagree with the claim that childhood obesity is not a problem in America today. When obese children become adults they may have a higher risk of developing deadly health problems that could have been prevented in childhood. Dr. Yung Seng Lee, a pediatric endocrinology specialist, believes that the rapid rise in childhood obesity around the world is the main cause for heart diseases, which affects the mortality rate of the human population. This means that too much fat in children can adversely affect their overall health. Dr. Lee also lists that a host of medical consequences are associated with childhood obesity, such as: glucose intolerance, dyslipidemia, hypertension, non-alcoholic fatty liver disease, polycystic ovarian syndrome, gallstones, obstructive sleep apnea, orthopedic disorders, and psuedotumour cerebri. All of these conditions were generally uncommon in children but have increased as childhood obesity rates have escalated. The fact that an obese child can develop these medical conditions illustrates that childhood obesity is in fact a serious problem in America.

In addition to a variety of health problems associated with obesity, the child will also be affected emotionally and socially. This is due to the excessive teasing of their peers from school and the sense that they are not accepted as part of the group. In Dr. Lee's view:

> Psychological and social consequences are probably more prevalent than medical complication. Childhood obesity has significant impact on the emotional development of the child or adolescent, who suffers discrimination . . . Individuals who were obese in childhood are more likely to have poor body image, and low self-esteem and confidence . . . as mid-childhood is the critical period of development of body image and self esteem . . . those with childhood obesity may have fewer opportunities in school, and a smaller social circle.

In other words, the excess weight the child carries will affect their overall physical health as adults. However, the emotional consequence that comes with childhood obesity is immediate and will impact the child through adulthood. Children will often make jokes at the expense of the overweight child, leaving the obese child feeling insecure about their body. Since this is a crucial time in a child's life where they learn to develop a sense of self-worth, having a poor image will affect them for the rest of their lives. Due to their lack of self-esteem most obese children will isolate themselves from social experiences, causing them to socially be less successful in life. Thus, the psychological effects are just as bad, if not worse, than the health effects an obese child will face as an adult.

Many nutritionists and dieticians argue that parents play a huge role in the childhood obesity epidemic. They argue that the child will eat whatever the parents cook or purchase at a drive-thru restaurant. The child has no other option but to consume the food their parents place in front of them, making the parents responsible for their child being overweight. Michelle Murphy Zive, a registered dietician, states:

> . . . a child learns what food to like, what to eat, when to eat, food rules and how much to eat in their environment which is largely 'controlled' by parents . . . It is critical that parents model and practice those eating habits that they want their child to learn, such as liking fruits and vegetables, snacking only when hungry and making a conscious effort to eat low, low caloric food . . . As parents you have the ability to purchase high-fat, high-sugar foods or not. (182–184)

The essence of Zive's argument is that parents are solely responsible for what their child eats. Children learn by example and parents need to set healthy rules about their child's eating habits. The child does not have the ability to go to the store and purchase unhealthy foods that can increase their chances for obesity. Since parents are the child's primary role model, they have the power to influence what their child eats on a day to day basis. Therefore, parents should set a good healthy example and be accountable for what their child eats.

Zive is correct when she argues the fact that parents control what their child consumes everyday. It is their sole responsibility to provide their child with healthy eating options at home and not purchase high fat, high calorie, and less nutritious foods. In her book, *Obesity*, Carrie Fredericks writes:

> If a parent has an unhealthy diet and gets little exercise, the chances are much greater that children in that household will also eat poorly and not exercise. It is almost impossible for a child to eat healthily if the parent does not, so the only way to correct this is to have the whole household eating healthy . . . "Teaching children about healthy habits requires the whole family's involvement; children are not going to learn these things on their own." (38)

To put it another way, children will learn and imitate what they see their parents doing, whether what they are doing is good or bad. This means that parents need to lead by example and show their children that they enjoy eating nutritious snacks and meals. By keeping healthy foods like apples, baby carrots, whole wheat crackers around the house the child will more likely choose to munch on those wholesome snacks. As a result, the child will be less likely to become obese because their parents have made a conscious effort to set a healthy example.

Moreover, children who are obese will more than likely be obese as adults. I believe that this will have an adverse effect in society because it has been shown that obese adults are less productive in the work place. Fredericks states:

> The cost of obesity related time off of work has increased dramatically . . . When employees do not feel well physically, they also might not perform their jobs to the best of their abilities. The U.S. Social Security Administration states that obesity increases the risk of developing physical impairments that would affect an individual's ability to complete everyday work tasks. Over 39 million workdays are lost every year due to obesity. (40)

Essentially, Fredericks' argument is that obese adults are less productive in their occupation due to some kind of physical health problem related to obesity. Mental health can also affect the productivity of an employee who is obese. As stated before, individuals who are obese often have low self-esteem and isolate themselves from social situations, causing them to miss work or not execute their work as effectively. If all the children who are obese today grow up as obese adults then we would have a community full of inefficient, unhealthy, insecure individuals running our society. Hence, obesity not only will affect the individual with that condition but society as well.

In conclusion, prevention of childhood obesity should be seen as a main priority in America. Childhood obesity is a growing problem in the United States and if obesity trends continue then more and more children will become obese in the next few years. Obesity has many negative effects on the child such as life threatening health problems, low self-esteem, anti-social, less productive as adults in the work place. The parent role is the most important in preventing obesity because they are their child's first teacher. The parents have the responsibility in educating their child on healthy eating habits because what they learn as children will stay with them as adults. These children will eventually become adults and we want the future leaders of country to be as confident, healthy (physically and mentally), and productive members of society.

Works Cited

Campos, Paul. *The Obesity Myth Why America's Obsession with Weight Is Hazardous to Your Health.* New York: Penguin Group, 2004. Print.

Fredericks, Carrie. *Obesity.* San Diego: Reference Point Inc., 2008. Print.

Fry, Elizabeth. "900-Pound Mother, Ruby, Obesity Rehab - Show Recap." *About.com.* About.com, 2010. Web. 1 Feb. 2010.

Lee, Yung Seng. "Consequences of Obesity." *NUS.* National University of Singapore, 2005. Web. 19 Jan. 2010.

"POP1 Child population: Number of children (in millions) ages 0–17 in the United States by age, 1950–2008 and projected 2009–2021." *ChildStats.gov Forum on Child and Family Statistics.* Federal Interagency Forum on Child and Family Statistics, 2008. Web. 1 Feb. 2010.

Zive, Michelle Murphy. "Parents Should Play a Role in Fighting Childhood Obesity." *Obesity Opposing Viewpoints.* Ed. Andrea C. Nakaya. San Francisco: Thomas Gale, 2006. 181–185. Print.

Name: _____

Questions

1. What is the author's main argument? What kind of claim is being made? Is this claim effective for this kind of essay? Explain.

_____

_____

_____

_____

_____

2. Analyze one of the support paragraphs. What kind of support is being used? Is the support effective? Are there any support paragraphs that are not effective?

_____

_____

_____

_____

_____

3. Discuss the introduction paragraph. Does the introduction hook the reader? Is the thesis clear and arguable? Explain.

_____

_____

_____

_____

_____

4. Discuss some of the essay's strengths. What does it do well? Be specific.

5. Does the essay have any weaknesses? Explain. How can these weaknesses be improved?

6. Do you agree or disagree with the author? Why? Be specific by referencing the essay. This answer may be written in the form of your own essay.

Samantha Zayas
English 68
February 17, 2011

One, Two, Three, No More Fast Food

The idea of someone else preparing and cooking the meal, while one is still able to eat the meal, has revolutionized people's diets. Since the first quick service restaurant opened in 1916, the fast food industry has growing tremendously, consequently, so has the obesity rate in America. As of 2009, sixty-three percent—about one hundred ninety-three million people—of the United State's population are obese (Hendrick). Obesity is a medical condition in which an individual's body weight is composed of more than twenty-five percent for male and thirty percent for female of fat (Powers and Dodd 170). With such high levels of fat, obese individuals have a higher risk for obesity-attributable diseases, such as coronary disease, stroke, hypertension, and certain cancers (Fiebelkorn, Finkelstein, and Wang 1). Among the many factors that can cause obesity, one factor is diet. Because American life is fast paced, most Americans do not have sufficient time to prepare and cook a healthy meal. Nonetheless, people still need to eat, and many have resorted to fast food restaurants to supply this need. Fast food is an unhealthy part of people's diet because fast food has unbalanced amounts of macronutrients[1], which can lead to obesity. Some nutrients are in large quantities and can provide unnecessary amounts of energy, while other nutrients, which can prevent obesity, are in small quantities. Because of fat food's unbalanced amounts of macronutrients, consuming fast food is unhealthy as it can lead to obesity.

The first reason fast food causes obesity is that it is high in protein. Protein should be the least consumed macronutrient. Fast food has unnecessary amounts of protein that, if not used, are stored in the body and are rarely uses once stored. This nutrient is abundantly found in animal products, which are usually the primary ingredient of fast food. The daily-recommended value for protein is twelve percent of one's caloric intake (Powers and Dodd 197). However, many American consume too much protein. Take the double patty cheeseburger with bacon from Carl Jr. as an example. It has fifty grams of protein ("Carl's, Jr. Cheeseburger, double patty, with bacon, sourdough, 10.5 oz."). Each gram of protein has four calories (Powers and Dodd 197). In a two thousand calorie diet, fifty grams of protein has two hundred calories and equates to ten percent of the diet. For an individual on such a diet, this is a sufficient daily amount. (The number of grams is subject variation to meet the caloric needs of a certain individual.) However, the average American does not eat one meal a day. By the end of the day, most people have consumed about twice the amount of protein that they should. Scott Powers and Stephen

---

[1] Macronutrients are nutrients such protein, fat, water, and carbohydrate that the human body requires in large quantities, in order to build and repair itself and maintain proper systemic function (Powers and Dodd 196).

Dodd are graduates from the University of Florida, are award-winning instructors with expertise in physiology, and are the authors of the book entitled *Total Fitness and Wellness*. They write the following about foods high in protein: "Because the average person in industrialized countries consumes more than enough protein, the nutritional problems associated with protein intake is one of excess . . . which can lead to an increased risk of heart disease, cancer, and obesity" (Powers and Dodd 203). Eating large amounts of protein can lead to obesity because the body cannot dispose of unused protein and is likely to store it. The purpose of protein in the body is to repair and build tissue, but if there is too much protein, the body is simply going to convert the used amount into glycogen to be amassed as extra body tissue. In extremely industrialized countries such as the United States, many people consume excessive amounts of protein from fast food daily. Gradually, they accumulate extensive amounts of it, to the point they become obese. Because protein is not needed in large amounts, eating too much of it can cause one's body to store protein.

Additionally, fast food contributes to obesity because it is high in triglycerides, or fats. Fat is a dense substance that has to be consumed in moderations, because it is difficultly for the body to utilize. However, this nutrient is easy for the body to store because the body does not have to convert fat into fat. There are three major types of triglycerides. Saturated fat and trans fat are a complex chain of molecules that are difficult to dissolve; meanwhile, unsaturated fat is a loose chain of molecules that are easy to break apart. In America, the majority of people exceed their daily amount—thirty percent of their caloric intake—of fat (Powers and Dodd 197). Fast food is unhealthy because the majority of the calories come from fat, specifically saturated. For example, a double patty cheeseburger with bacon from Carl's Jr. has a total of fifty-nine grams of triglycerides ("Carl's, Jr. Cheeseburger, double patty, with bacon, sourdough, 10.5 oz."). Twenty-four grams are saturated fat, and the remaining fat is unknowingly distributed between trans fat and unsaturated fat. Per gram, there are nine calories (Powers and Dodd 199). Based on a two thousand calorie diet, this cheeseburger has five hundred thirty-one calories of fat. With twenty-seven percent of the daily value, the burger from Carl's Jr. contains enough fat that a person on a two thousand calorie diet should consume, and this does not include side dishes, such as French fries and fried onion rings. Usually, people do not use all the energy they attain from fast food meals. Therefore, their body stores the unburned triglycerides for later use, progressively increasing their body's storage of fat. The authors of *Total Fitness and Wellness* write, "Both saturated and unsaturated fats are linked to heart disease, obesity, and certain cancers" (Powers and Dodd 206). Consuming large amounts of fat can be extremely unhealthy. Despite the type of fat consumed, people who eat fatty foods are likely to become obesity because the body quickly stores excess fat, since the body does not have to convert this nutrient. As stated above, fast food, in particular, is deleterious because it is mainly composed of fat. Many Americans consume more than the daily-recommended thirty percent, which has caused many of them to becoming obese. Consuming excess amounts of fat is not good because one's body is going to store most of the fat readily, since fat is easy to store.

Moreover, fast food is an attributor of obesity because it has little to no water. Water is important because it decreases fat deposit in one's body. With a reduced fat content, people have a lower probability of becoming obese. The function of water is to aids the kidneys in excreting waste from the body. If there is a shortage of water, the liver assists the kidneys. The purpose of the liver is to convert stored fat into energy for the body to use. If it is helping the kidneys, the liver is not able to properly regulate the body's metabolism. As a result, the liver does not work at its full potential, therefore, making the individual gain weight. People who eat fast food do not usually consume sufficient water. In fact, in the nutrition label of the double patty cheeseburger with bacon from Carl's Jr., the researchers did not calculate or even attempt to estimate the possible amount of water that there can be in this fast food item. Beside the word "water", there is simply a question mark—the place where a percentage is usually found ("Carl's, Jr. Cheeseburger, double patty, with bacon, sourdough, 10.5 oz"). This implies that there is no water content in the burger. The daily-recommended amount of water is eight to ten glasses (Balch 108). Even though people's daily amount of water is subject to variation, most people who consistently eat fast food do not drink adequate amount of water that their body, especially their kidneys, needs to function properly. According to *The Colon Therapists Network*, an organization focused on educating people by providing them with important information on the human body, "Water . . . helps the body metabolize stored fat. Studies have shown that a *decrease* in water intake will cause fat deposits to *increase*" ("The Water Health Report: How eight glasses a day keeps the fat off!"). Not drinking plenty amounts of water can lead to weight gain and eventually obesity. When people's bodies lack water, they do not have the highest metabolism possible. Instead, they force their liver to multitask, when it could and should be concentrating on maximizing their metabolism. Although drinking water can increase the metabolism rate, many Americans ignore water. They prefer to consume burgers, sodas, and other fast food items that are not a significant source of water. Hence, they can slowly become obese. In order to reduce fat deposits in the body, one has to consume adequate amount of water, which can also reduces one's possibility of obesity.

Finally, fast food leads to obesity because it is low in fiber. Fiber, a type of carbohydrate, is an important part of people's diet because fiber can prevent people from overeating. By not overeating, people have a lower chance of become obese. There are two types of fiber, soluble, which aids in controlling appetite, and insoluble, which helps increase the time required for the food to pass through the intestinal track (Balch 9). Slowing down the rate at which food travels in the intestines creates the long lasting feeling of a satisfied hunger. Because the human body cannot digest fiber and simply excrete it, fiber does not have a caloric value (Balch 10). Therefore, eating too much fiber cannot cause a person to become obese. As an example, in the double patty cheeseburger with bacon from Carl's Jr., there are only two grams of dietary fiber ("Carl's, Jr. Cheeseburger, double patty, with bacon, sourdough, 10.5 oz"). The minimum daily-recommended amount of fiber to consume is twenty-five grams (Powers and Dodd 198). It would take thirteen double cheeseburgers to reach the minimum recommendation.

However, with that many burgers, a person would also eat eleven thousand four hundred forty calories and eight hundred fifteen grams of fat, which is extremely bad for one's health and can increase one's chances of obesity. According to the researchers at the University of Maryland Medical Center, "[C]linical studies and human case reports suggest that soluble fiber . . . may make you feel full and less hungry, so that you eat less and lose weight" (Zieve and Eltz). Fiber is important to combat weight gain and preventing obesity because it creates lasting, satisfied hunger. People who eat fiber consume fewer excess calories, which place these people at a lower risk for obesity than other who eat insufficient amounts of fiber. Consequently, fast foods contain small trace of fiber; thus, people who eat fast food are likely to become obese. Fiber is essential to have in one's diet because fiber can prevent obesity by reducing one's chances of overeating.

To recapitulate, the fast food diet, which many Americans enjoy on a regularly basis, is unhealthy because it can lead to obesity. First, fast food is extremely high in protein. The double patty cheeseburger with bacon has ten percent of the daily value of protein a person on a two thousand calories diet should consume. In addition, fast food is high in fat. The Carl's Jr. burger that was used as an example has fifty-nine grams of fat, enough to meet one's daily needs if on a two thousand calorie diet. Unlike the other two nutrients, fast food has almost no water, as in the Carl's Jr. burger example. Water reduces the fat storage in the body, decreasing one's chances of becoming obese, but for this to occur, one has to consume eight to ten large glasses of water. Furthermore, fast food is low in fiber. The burger example has only two grams of fiber. In order to have an enduring satisfied hunger and prevent obesity, one has to consume at least twenty-five grams of fiber daily. Ultimately, fast food is deleterious to consume because it can lead to obesity. The next time one craves a Carl's Jr. double patty cheeseburger with bacon or any other fast food item, study the nutritional facts of the fast food item. Determine whether the meal in scrutiny is a balanced source of fats, protein, fiber, and water so that the meal contains a portion of one's daily-recommended amounts of macronutrients. If it has too much fat and protein and too little water and fiber, reconsider what to have for a meal. If it is an unbalanced meal, similar to the Carl's Jr. double patty cheeseburger with bacon, the meal will probably increase one's possibility of gaining large amounts of excess fat. One will most likely be amazed to discover how fatty, proteinous, waterless, and fiberless (simply unhealthy) fast food is, and because of this, fast food can unmistakably lead to obesity. Most meals on fast food menu have unbalanced amounts of macronutrients, which make these fast food items potential attributors of obesity.

Works Cited

Balch, Phyllis A. *Prescription for nutritional healing: the A-to-Z guide to supplements.* New York: Avery, 2010. Print.

"Carl's, Jr. Cheeseburger, double patty, with bacon, sourdough, 10.5 oz." *Fast Food Nutrition.* DietPower Inc., 2011. Web. 2 Feb. 2011.

Files, JD. "Fast Food History in America." *Ezine Articles.* EzineArticles.com, 2011. Web. 4 Feb. 2011.

Finkelstein, Eric A., Ian C. Fiebelkorn, and Guijing Wang. "National Medical Spending Attributable to Overweight and Obesity in the United States: How Much, and Who's Paying." *Health Affairs.* Project HOPE: The People-to-People Health Foundation Inc., 14 May 2003. Web. 18 Jan. 2011.

Hendrick, Bill. "Percentage of Overweight, Obese Americans Swells Americans Are Eating Poorly, Exercising Less, and Getting Bigger, Survey Finds." *WebMD.* WebMD, LLC., 2011. Web. 4 Feb. 2011.

Powers, Scott K. and Stephen L. Dodd. *Total Fitness and Wellness.* 5th ed. California: Benjamin-Cummings Publishing Company, 2008. Print.

"The Water Health Report: How eight glasses a day keeps the fat off!" *The Colon Therapists Network.* The Colon Therapists Network, 2010. Web. 4 Feb. 2010.

Zieve, David and David R. Eltz. "Fiber." *University of Maryland Medical Center.* University of Maryland Medical Center, 2006. Web. 2 Feb. 2011.

Name: _____

Questions

1. What is the author's main argument? What kind of claim is being made? Is this claim effective for this kind of essay? Explain.

   _____

   _____

   _____

   _____

   _____

2. Analyze one of the support paragraphs. What kind of support is being used? Is the support effective? Are there any support paragraphs that are not effective?

   _____

   _____

   _____

   _____

   _____

3. Discuss the introduction paragraph. Does the introduction hook the reader? Is the thesis clear and arguable? Explain.

   _____

   _____

   _____

   _____

4. Discuss some of the essay's strengths. What does it do well? Be specific.

_____

_____

_____

_____

_____

5. Does the essay have any weaknesses? Explain. How can these weaknesses be improved?

_____

_____

_____

_____

_____

6. Do you agree or disagree with the author? Why? Be specific by referencing the essay. This answer may be written in the form of your own essay.

_____

_____

_____

_____

_____

Kevin Russell
English 1C
1-26-12

A Government's Role in Overcoming Obesity

Many Americans believe that the consumers are to blame for, what the Surgeon General calls, the obesity epidemic. While they rarely admit as much, consumers often take for granted that they have a choice in what they put into their bodies. Similarly, many believe it is not the government's responsibility to protect us from food companies. Our government should not need to force the food industry to stop selling unhealthy food because some people choose to overindulge. In his essay "What You Eat Is Your Business," Radley Balko agrees when he writes, "Instead of manipulating or intervening in the array of food options available to American consumers, our government ought to be working to foster a sense of responsibility in and ownership of our own health and well-being" (158). He believes our government should pass off the responsibility of being healthy to the consumers. Conventional wisdom has it that obesity has detrimental health effects, but with just a little self-control and personal responsibility, Americans can control whether or not they become obese. Accordingly, the government does not need to regulate the food companies in America.

While the consumer does have a choice as to what they eat, the government still needs to regulate food companies. By focusing on the consumer, Balko overlooks the deeper problem of the extremely unhealthy food readily available to them. Most restaurants do not disclose the nutritional information at the time of purchase, thus preventing their customers to make logical decisions on what is healthy enough for them to eat. This makes it difficult for a consumer of a restaurant's food to eat responsibly. In an article on the internet written by Stone Phillips, John Banzhaf, a law professor at George Washington University, offers his opinion:

> Banzhaf hopes lawsuits will force the fast food industry to disclose, on the menu board, just how fattening the food is. Restaurants don't have to list calories like packaged food do, but Banzhaf says they should. He also wants it to be required that fast food outlets offer more nutritious alternatives. And he wants health warnings to greet you every time you pull up or walk in to order.

If the government made it so health warnings and nutritional information were provided, it would help customers to determine what is healthy at restaurants. In addition, if restaurants had nutritious alternatives on their menu, consumers would then have the opportunity to make these healthy food choices. At this point, the responsible choices discussed earlier can then be made. In the same article by Stone Phillips, Banzhaf furthers his argument by stating, "It's hard to believe that just over the last 20 years, which is when this epidemic started, that somehow we all lost personal responsibility." Since the chances of all obese Americans losing their personal responsibility are slim, perhaps the food served at restaurants has become unhealthier. Maybe the food industries' bombardment of advertisements for their unhealthy food caused the rise in obesity. One thing is certain however, without government intervention, the obesity epidemic will remain an issue.

Works Cited

Balko, Radley. "What You Eat Is Your Business." *They Say I Say: With Readings.* Gerald Graff, Cathy Birkenstein, and Russel Durst. New York: W. W. Norton & Company, Inc., 2009. 157–160. Print.

Phillips, Stone. "Who's to blame for the U.S. obesity epidemic?" *msn.* msnbc.com, 2006. Web. 24 Jan. 2012.

Name: _____

Questions

1. What is the author's main argument? What is the overall claim being made? Explain.

   _____

   _____

   _____

   _____

   _____

2. Analyze one of the paragraphs. What kind of support is being used? Is the support effective?

   _____

   _____

   _____

   _____

   _____

3. Discuss the flow of one of the paragraphs. Is the topic sentence effective? Does the rest of the paragraph match the topic sentence? Explain.

   _____

   _____

   _____

   _____

   _____

4. Discuss some of the strengths of this assignment. What does it do well? Be specific.

5. Does the assignment have any weaknesses? Explain. How can these weaknesses be improved?

6. Do you agree or disagree with the author? Why? Be specific by referencing the essay. This answer may be written in the form of your own essay.

Wylie McGraw
English 101
30 June 2011

Obesity and America Today

Can you imagine what it would be like if the entire population of America was obese and life expectancy was shorter than that of previous generations by as much as twenty to thirty years? With a country vigorous at overpopulating communities with fast food restaurants and the idea that people do not have time anymore for a sit down healthy meal, that question may not be far off from a reality. Playing on the fast paced and technologically advanced society in America today, fast food has become second nature, for most Americans, as a primary choice in nutrition. That is scary. To think that America has been improving over this past generation is naïve at the least. To believe that in the last decade changes have been for the greater good of Americans is downright ignorant. If the people in the United States continue on the path of laziness, we will see, without a doubt, the complete disruption of life expectancy for humans on a global level. People will die at younger ages from more serious health complications. Without intervention and some sort of leadership, our children do not stand a fighting chance at a future.

Fast food restaurants are marketing their products in valiant effort to lure the younger age groups into what businesses call "brand name preference." Children are psychologically too young to understand the purpose of advertisement and that is exactly what the marketing officials for major fast food chains are banking on. The men and women who run the ads for places, like McDonald's, have been known to hire psychologists to help mold the perfect commercial to a child's likes. Children simply take what they see at face value and love bright, shiny things. Eric Schlosser, an investigative journalist, makes clear in his essay, "Your Trusted Friends", from the *They Say/I Say: with Readings*, about the founder of *McDonald's* and his perfecting of the art of selling to children. He says, "Promoting McDonald's to children was a clever, pragmatic decision" (Schlosser 186). As the founder of McDonald's, Ray A. Kroc exclaims, "A child who loves our TV commercials and brings her grandparents to a McDonald's gives us two more customers" (Schlosser 186). Schlosser goes on to state, "A person's 'brand loyalty' may begin as early as the age of two . . . children often recognize a brand logo before they can recognize their own name" (190). This comes from how the advertisers are working with children. They need to study a child's taste before they can manipulate their behavior and they study a child's fantasy life, then design their products and apply those findings into advertisements (Schlosser 190). This all seems a cruel and unfair manner to conduct business. Business owners are so intent on profit margins; they will stoop to any level in order for economic superiority. That includes crippling the health and welfare of future generations, but it works and kids are "eating it up," while their parents support it and thank it for making their lives easier. What about the lives of your children?

However, certain experts disagree with what Americans call an "obesity epidemic" and feel it is a matter of a set standard for body mass index that puts most healthy people in the "obese" or "overweight category. What is commonly heard is that more than 60% of Americans are obese, when in reality "more than 60% of Americans are 'overweight' and 25% are 'obese,' we need to first understand how these terms are being defined" (J. Eric Oliver 14). J. Eric Oliver is a political scientist who wrote the book *Fat Politics: The Real Story behind America's Obesity Epidemic*. He says, "In America, being labeled or perceived as overweight means your life will be harder on a number of fronts . . . you will receive different medical care. In some cases you may be denied a job" (Oliver 14). The designation of overweight or obese hits the core of an individual's identity. Oliver goes on to argue, "How these terms get defined ultimately depends on who gains from making people concerned about their body size and who has an interest in getting people to try to lose weight" (15). Americans are being labeled and the only reason behind it is a few "experts" made up [standards] for what normal weight should be. According to the author, "The primary reason why 60% of Americans are 'overweight' has nothing to do with fast-food, cars, or television . . . these definitions have little to do with scientific evidence about weight and health and a lot to do with simple mathematics, insurance premiums, and the pecuniary (money) interests of the pharmaceutical industry" (Oliver 16). That means Americans are caught up in yet another vicious scheme of manipulation for profit. People are being led to believe that fast-food is the leading issue with "obesity" and it seems that the facts are being overlooked, or better yet, clouded by the money the lies generate.

To think, being "obese" or "overweight" is merely a hollow definitive word concocted by a group of intellects for the purpose of a profitable ploy, could mislead a reader into believing fast-food does not contribute to excess weight or health issues related to living with that weight. The products found in today's typical fast-food locations are as healthy as smoking a cigarette. Both cause long term damage to the body that tends to go unnoticed for a good majority of an individual's life. The sugar that is packed into these food products not only appeases the taste bud, but also supersedes what the human body should naturally intake on a daily basis. Sugar is addicting and has been connected to many health related ailments, such as diabetes, a disease where the body cannot respond to the insulin produced or does not produce enough of it. Insulin is what assists moving nutrients into the cells of the body. Heart diseases, high blood pressure, and high cholesterol are some of the other serious health risks associated with poor nutrition. Fast-food consists of processed materials, usually loaded with high concentrations of saturated fats, and prepared through unconventional means like microwaves and electric grills. Most Americans eat like this every day of the week, sometimes multiple times a day, and are exposing their children to it at a young age, an age where the body is still developing and requires proper nutrition to become optimal. Combined with little to no actual physical activity because Americans are consumed with video games and the internet, the body will not digest the fats, sugars, and processed carbohydrates, instead storing them within the body as more of a defense mechanism against starvation. When the body feels that it is not acquiring its necessary dose of nutrition, it begins to store fat as a way to supplement an energy source in order for it to survive. It can be said that different cultures define what truly is "overweight" and "obese," that Americans label and stereotype for the purpose of a profit; however, look at it any way desirable, without exercise to burn off the processed garbage fast-food consists of, people will continue to grow in size and weight dragging along with them the possibility that their bodies may develop a disease that could eventually kill them at a very young age. What is more startling; children have no choice in the matter when parents now are more to blame than any corporation is. Packing unnatural and unhealthy materials into young, developing bodies stunts the growth patterns necessary for a long and prosperous life. With a health care system that is broken and an inflated price tag, future generations will not get to enjoy their lives, but rather pay dearly for them because of their poor choices in nutrition.

In the end, people need to make better choices when it comes to their food. Too much sugar and fat can cause extreme health problems throughout a person's life. The biggest concern that lurks with eating fast-food is obesity and the disease that obesity contributes to is typically diabetes or heart problems. The fast-food industry has saturated the country with saturated fats and its marketing towards children is misleading. Health care costs have doubled over the past 30 years and the poorer communities suffer the most. There must be a cultural change in the way Americans view and consume food. Parents need to teach their children about health and nutrition, leading by example. Without proper education, many more will continue to suffer and the obesity crisis will never stop "growing."

Works Cited

Oliver, J. Eric. *Fat Politics: The Real Story behind America's Obesity Epidemic*. Oxford: Oxford Press, 2006. Print.

Schlosser, Eric. "Your Trusted Friends." *They Say/I Say: with Readings*. Gerald Graff, Cathy Birkenstein, and Russell Durst. New York: W.W. Norton & Company, 2009. Print.

Name: _____

Questions

1. What is the author's main argument? What kind of claim is being made? Is this claim effective for this kind of essay? Explain.

   _____

   _____

   _____

   _____

   _____

2. Analyze one of the support paragraphs. What kind of support is being used? Is the support effective? Are there any support paragraphs that are not effective?

   _____

   _____

   _____

   _____

   _____

3. Discuss the introduction paragraph. Does the introduction hook the reader? Is the thesis clear and arguable? Explain.

   _____

   _____

   _____

   _____

   _____

4. Discuss some of the essay's strengths. What does it do well? Be specific.

_____

_____

_____

_____

_____

5. Does the essay have any weaknesses? Explain. How can these weaknesses be improved?

_____

_____

_____

_____

_____

6. Do you agree or disagree with the author? Why? Be specific by referencing the essay. This answer may be written in the form of your own essay.

_____

_____

_____

_____

_____

Chapter 13

The Military

America's military power is one of the strongest in the world. Our soldiers are deployed in all kinds of regions and fight for all kinds of reasons. In some cases, our military is also the "face" of our country, which is why it sparks so many different debates in public forums. Although both combo paragraphs in this chapter are about the military, neither assignment is related to the other. Jessica Yazdani argues about the Obama Administration's choice to continue to fight in Afghanistan, while Maggie Le discusses gays in the military and the recent "don't ask, don't tell" controversies.

Jessica Yazdani
English 1C
1.16.12

The Fight for Political Freedom

The Obama Administration asserts that continuing to stay in the war in Afghanistan is necessary in order to stabilize the corrupt government there. The United States government believes that even though we have not yet won the war, we have made progress towards creating a stable economy in the country of Afghanistan. Laws such as the Sharia Law are enforced in Afghanistan by the Taliban people. This law forces women to be fully covered in clothing from head to toe. They are denied to health care, education, they are forbidden to laugh loudly, speak loudly, and even walk noisily. (Johnson). The Taliban without any court or hearings will cut people's arms or hands off when accused of stealing. They watch the streets and conduct brutal public beatings daily (Johnson). These acts occur in Afghanistan under Taliban control. However, the Obama Administration asserts that the United States being in war with Afghanistan has been able to reduce the amount of power that the Taliban people hold. At one point, the Taliban held 90 percent of control over Afghanistan (Bajoria). Since the United States has been in war with Afghanistan, we have been able to eliminate much of the Taliban leaders. For example, the United States NATO forces have had success in killing or capturing Taliban leaders since the start of the war. A U.S. air strike in December of 2006 killed Mullah Akhtar Usmani, a top commander. In May 2007, coalition forces killed the leader of the Taliban insurgency in the south, his name was Mullah Dadullah (Bajoria). Killing important leaders such as these is weakening the Taliban control. The Obama administration believes that pulling out of the war will lead to the Taliban to return to power and will continue to rule the country in horrendous ways. To conclude, the Obama administration feels that staying in the war with Afghanistan is the only way the individuals living there have a chance of living a life without destruction. I agree with the decision that the Obama administration has made in staying in the Afghanistan war. Ending the war now would be the wrong thing to do. If the U.S. decided to leave the war, this would cause the U.S. to be vulnerable in being attacked by the Taliban. The Taliban people will be able to create terrorist training camps. This could eventually lead to attacks on U.S. soil. According to an internet article, these camps train 1,000 to 1,500 Taliban people at a time, all of which are capable of increasing and strengthening their weapons, intelligence, and plan to attack the United States ("Afghanistan-Militia Facilities"). On October 7 2001, the U.S. commenced an assault on the Taliban state in Afghanistan, which allowed Bin Laden to train terrorist followers and to plan as well as facilitate attacks from inside Afghanistan (Griff 11). This terrorist sanctuary was eliminated, in order for the U.S. and world community to be safe from future acts of violence. This war has kept training camps from spreading. In fact, it is reported in an article that, "Under Taliban protection, Al Qaida established a number of training camps in Afghanistan, however, most were destroyed in the international military action by the U.S." ("Terrorist Training and Indoctrination"). If the United States was not working hard to ensure the spread of these camps from happening, the U.S. would be in great danger. As a result, this war is now mandatory for protection for United State citizens. We have already gotten rid of many training camps in Afghanistan and by doing so; we are minimizing the Taliban power. Finally, I feel that it is important to keep fighting the war in Afghanistan because the Taliban people are ruthless and they should not be in control any longer. Their training camps must be demolished to prevent future attacks from occurring.

Works Cited

"Afghanistan-Militia Facilities." *Global Security.org.* Global Security.org, 2012. Web. 17 Jan. 2012.

Bajoria, Jayshree. "The Taliban in Afghanistan." *Counsel on Foreign Relations.* Counsel on Foreign Relations, 2011. Web 17 Jan. 2012.

Griff, Witte. *Overcoming The Obstacles to Establishing a Democratic State in Afghanistan.* Washington: Washington Post, 24 Feb. 2007. Print.

Johnson, Toni. "Islam: Governing Under Sharia." *Counsel on Foreign Relations.* Counsel on Foreign Relations, 2011. Web. 16 Jan. 2012.

"Terrorist Training and Indoctrination." *Security Service MI 5.* Security Service MI 5, 2011. Web. 17 Jan. 2012. <https://www.mi5.gov.uk/output/terrorist-training.html>.

Name: _____

Questions

1. What is the author's main argument? What is the overall claim being made? Explain.

_____

_____

_____

_____

_____

2. Analyze one of the paragraphs. What kind of support is being used? Is the support effective?

_____

_____

_____

_____

_____

3. Discuss the flow of one of the paragraphs. Is the topic sentence effective? Does the rest of the paragraph match the topic sentence? Explain.

_____

_____

_____

_____

_____

4. Discuss some of the strengths of this assignment. What does it do well? Be specific.

_____

_____

_____

_____

_____

5. Does the assignment have any weaknesses? Explain. How can these weaknesses be improved?

_____

_____

_____

_____

6. Do you agree or disagree with the author? Why? Be specific by referencing the essay. This answer may be written in the form of your own essay.

_____

_____

_____

_____

Maggie Le
English 1C
1-19-12

Gays in the Military

When the sensitive topic of homosexuality arises, a majority of people would readily agree that homosexuals deserve to have the same equal rights that heterosexuals do. Where this agreement usually ends, however, is on the question of whether men, of a gay sexual orientation, should be allowed to participate in the military like a heterosexual man can. Critics may argue and evidently agree that in "section 571 of the law describes homosexuality in the ranks as an 'unacceptable risk . . . to morale, good order, and discipline'" ("Homosexuals in the Military" 104). Those who believe that gays should not participate in the military reject the idea of change in traditional structure because they fear that the exposure of homosexuality in the military would jeopardize the armed forces from properly serving their country. Some are convinced that having gays in the military will disrupt the sense of personal security for others and corrupt the social structure of the military. An individual's sexual orientation greatly influences the standards of qualification to engage in the armed forces due to the fear of interference military structure of order, command to authority, organization, and cooperation as a joint force.

Morality plays a big role on the determination of allowing gays into the military, but people who want to join, regardless of their sexual orientation, deserve to receive the same treatment. A soldier's sexual orientation would not affect the capability or performance to train, learn, or fight for his country; physical ability and emotional attractions do not interact with one another. Hill agrees when he writes that "such strength begins with accepting that everyone is unique and equally integral to the whole." (47). He portrays the idea of remaining and working together as a whole even with all the differences between each soldier. If the soldiers can cooperate and efficiently accomplish what they need to get done, they would be proudly serving their country. A person's right to join the military should not be taken away due to the poor judgment of the sexual preference, but for the lack of ability to serve his country as a soldier.

Works Cited

Hill, Robert M. "Soldiers All." *Military Review*. 91. 6 (2011): 46–48. Print.

"Homosexuals in the Military." *Congressional Digest*. 89. 4 (2010): 103–107. Print.

Name: _____

Questions

1. What is the author's main argument? What is the overall claim being made? Explain.

   _____

   _____

   _____

   _____

   _____

2. Analyze one of the paragraphs. What kind of support is being used? Is the support effective?

   _____

   _____

   _____

   _____

   _____

3. Discuss the flow of one of the paragraphs. Is the topic sentence effective? Does the rest of the paragraph match the topic sentence? Explain.

   _____

   _____

   _____

   _____

   _____

4. Discuss some of the strengths of this assignment. What does it do well? Be specific.

5. Does the assignment have any weaknesses? Explain. How can these weaknesses be improved?

6. Do you agree or disagree with the author? Why? Be specific by referencing the essay. This answer may be written in the form of your own essay.